The Natural Garden

To Sophie Lee, artist, dancer and little mother;
Jacob, scientist and digger of dinosaur bones;
their father, my always; Juma, our high chief, cook
and clown; and Grandpa, the Sufi of Rapuke Moana.

The Natural Garden

Landscape Ideas for New Zealand Gardens

Xanthe White

GODWIT

7

PREFACE

17

THE NATURAL
Flower Garden

43

THE NATURAL
Subtropical Garden

71

THE NATURAL
Productive Garden

101

THE NATURAL
Rooftop Garden

119

THE NATURAL
Restored Garden

145

THE NATURAL
Coastal Garden

171

THE NATURAL
Dry Garden

195

THE NATURAL
Country Garden

221

THE NATURAL
Beekeeper's Garden

235

THE NATURAL
Native Garden

261

THE NATURAL
Small Garden

285

THE NATURAL
Collector's Garden

295

THE NATURAL
Gardener

I can't quite remember when I first came across a wonderful, ancient book called *The Wild Garden*, first published in Britain in 1870 by William Robinson, who, during his life and through various editions of his book, added to his gardening philosophy as his ideas developed and matured.

His approach influenced many of his garden-design and horticulturalist contemporaries but its greatest impact, and relevance, has been during this modern period of gardening history. Robinson was ahead of his time — or perhaps we have just caught up with him. Either way, he believed plants should be left as much in their natural form as possible, naturalised into the landscape rather than being collected and tamed and planted into the colour blocks that were the practice of his era. Planting a 'wild', or natural, garden is in some ways a more complex approach to gardening as it requires a specific knowledge of each site and a broad understanding of the vast kingdom of plants. But the gardens that exemplify this approach are both easier to maintain and are also the most sustainable response we can make to our landscapes.

It's common in gardening and landscape architecture and design circles to have debate whether natives or exotics should be used in our gardens. It's an important discussion to have. One side of the argument champions the exclusive use of native flora, on the grounds that they are the treasures of our cultural heritage and that they also have a functional value. But within exotic species there is also diversity and complexity to treasure. We need to be careful with it, however. Our native flora is utterly unique, and despite the centuries of human

Preface

▲ **PREVIOUS PAGES** I planted purple flowering thyme to blend through *Santolina chamaecyparissus* 'Green Fizz' in the courtyard garden at Dalton's Plantation gardens. Even in the natural garden continuity and repetition are important.

▶ **RIGHT** The texture in this planting at Dalton's comes from New Zealand natives *Chionochloa flavicans, Anemanthele lessoniana* and the endangered *Carmichaelia* (native broom) while the exotic flowers (burgundy Iceberg, helenium and armeria) and the leaves of *Cercis canadensis* (forest pansy) frame the path and help highlight otherwise subtle tones.

habitation of Aotearoa, still not fully explored. There is enough complexity in our native plant material that one person's dedicated gardening life could never exhaust. Rather, it will take generations of plantspeople to truly understand its intricacies.

Nothing — especially nature — is black or white, and all plants should be valued for their appropriateness to a site, and their potential to do good in preserving the diversity and complexity of our world. While preserving nature we also need to understand that it is constantly changing, and that the impact we have had on the landscape is part of that metamorphosis. The best approach, surely, is to utilise the complexity of both natives and exotics. The home gardener's response to his or her immediate habitat is significant; in other words, gardening is so much more than a hobby. It's an active contributor to the balance of the environment around us. Growing heirloom varieties in the vegetable garden, for example, contributes to the preservation of varieties that may be the plants of the future given that changing climatic conditions will no doubt dictate what we can grow. Flowers, to use another example, are critically important to insect and bird life, and are an essential link for pollinators such as bees.

Native plants, too, should be celebrated as an important part of gardens not just because they enable us to create a perfectly managed natural ecosystem in our backyards but also because they help support the complex natural web on which we depend. However, gardeners should be expansive about the natives they plant, not settling for municipal-style plantings of cabbage trees and flax (both of which I love, I hasten to add) but rather looking to new and different varieties, combining them with exotics where appropriate.

> While preserving nature we also need to understand that it is constantly changing, and that the impact we have had on the landscape is part of that metamorphosis.

AS WILLIAM ROBINSON argued, our gardens should be celebrations of the complexities of nature not rows of monocultures that mimic architecture in their rigidity. But how do we let nature into our gardens without unleashing chaos? It's as much about what we don't do as about what we do do. Reducing the use of sprays and other chemicals can have its frustrations but doing so allows nature to find its own remedies. Limiting or resiling from spray use also prevents damage to bee populations and to the many small creatures that inhabit healthy gardens. We can assist nature by deciding to plant hedges rather than build fences and walls; after all, it's far cheaper and if you plant mature hedging plants privacy can be attained relatively quickly.

The natural gardener abhors the straight line. To be sure, lines are useful when it comes to construction and for creating clearly defined boundaries, but it is possible to let go of a rigid structure in order to create spaces that are more suited to the natural forms of a site. While the easiest solution may seem, at first, to be to level and square a site, it is often much more pleasing — and affordable — to allow a gentle slope to remain, using curves to form connected spaces that can wiggle into corners. The curve can also create a satisfying tension between the straight lines of our buildings and the wild plants that surround them. When you exploit nature's curves and add layers of planting, you are sculpting spaces that can be sublime. If a site is close to a source of local stone, all the better. With the placement of rock in a naturalistic way you can create and change levels without having to build costly, and often unattractive, retaining walls.

Nor does the wild, or natural, garden lack rules or order. Just as it's almost unknown in nature to find plants dotted in rows, so it should be in our gardens. Repetition, achieved through sweeps of planting, is essential. As well as highlights, gardens need simple, pleasing drifts of plants otherwise we become overwhelmed by complexity.

Nor should function be an accidental. As with all design, the use and purpose of a space should be defined before the plants are placed around it. The spaces through and on which we move should have a different rhythm to those where we sit, and outdoor dining spaces

▶ **RIGHT** You need to consider the final heights of different flowering perennial varieties. Cleome can be grown from seed but will tower over you. Cannas are great for the back of borders, and autumn sedum, foxgloves and catmint can happily mingle.

should be paved appropriately. When they are sited close to the house they are perhaps best kept squared, connected to the architecture of the house rather than to the garden. As spaces become less formal, the surfaces may become more broken as nature weaves its way in. The real complexity occurs in the cracks and the crevices, and in the 'accidents' that we as gardeners allow to happen.

All landscape designers come, over time, to have a signature style. It took me some time to realise that mine had come to sit firmly within William Robinson's 'wild', or natural, garden approach. That realisation now informs all the decisions I make when I begin work in a new project. Early in my career I was much more focused on the built structure of a garden; walls and paths came first, the plants later. Now my approach is plant-driven first and foremost.

Landscape design is most importantly about plantmanship. As gardens have become increasingly 'low maintenance' it has been fashionable to limit plants, so much so that many gardens may have as few as one, two, perhaps three varieties. Sometimes, particularly in small spaces, this has been done very well, but often it has simply stripped the joy from our gardens. For it is plants that bring magic to our outdoor spaces and it's the joy of gardening that makes landscape design such a pleasure. Unlike other fields of design, the end results are not completely controlled by us. Nature also has a say. Plants have minds of their own, wandering in another direction from what was planned or perhaps not flowering in the predicted colour. Nor does our work ever stay the same. Small trees grow big; where there was sun there will be shade. Large trees get tired and collapse or are removed from neighbours' properties, opening up sky and sun but also perhaps the view of an unsightly garden shed. Our work is constantly at work.

While this could be seen as a frustration, it is really the joy of a garden. It's a constant process of change, into which come moments of perfection, when everything in the garden lights up, when it becomes an orchestrated marriage of colour and form. It's these moments the plant lover works for. It is as much about artistry as it is about design.

My intention with this book is to show you the magic of plants,

and how, through careful planning, they can transform the mundane into the extraordinary. Although I've spent more than half my life in the field, I'm still an apprentice in awe of the masters. The greats like Piet Oudolf and Patrick Blanc lead the game with a vast understanding of plants and of how they can be brought into our cities, and tamed in our gardens. Both these designers have a crisp confidence to their work, but their plant palettes are rich and complex. The results are exquisite.

To really learn about plants you have to grow them. My home garden is small and overflowing with experiments. For this reason it has been such a wonderful commission to be given a piece of land near Matamata on which I can unleash my creativity. I've learnt a lot as I've created the Dalton's Plantation gardens. A blank piece of land is hard to garden; there's no shade, and pastureland is like a desert environment when it comes to retaining water during a hot summer. And until Judith Dalton invited me to be part of this project I had little experience with real frosts — the ones that freeze your water features over! From developing the productive gardens which supply the café, to planting out the deep flower beds and working with the rich palette of native plant material, I've taken as my inspiration the many incredible gardens I've seen on my travels, including in Japan, and have endeavoured to bring those same aesthetic values to life with our own unique plant palette. Like all gardens it's a work in progress, but those moments of beauty are already appearing. And they are simply addictive.

In this book, I explain how many styles of gardens can be designed and maintained according to the natural garden principles. Those principles don't constitute a firm set of rules. They are more like a spirit, and they give gardeners enormous creativity and flexibility. I hope you will come to be inspired.

Xanthe White

THE NATURAL
Flower
Garden

A flower garden is not something New Zealanders associate with wildness or naturalness. Instead we think of our grandmothers and the influence of English colonisation. Yet the original concept of the wild garden came from the Irish gardener William Robinson, whose naturalistic ideals greatly influenced the great flower gardeners such as Gertrude Jekyll, who was his dear friend. His ideal was of a garden suited to place and driven by function as well as beauty. His philosophy lines up with modern views of ecology: the wild flower garden was not high maintenance but instead a combination of plants, suited to their locations, that would then naturalise and flourish.

OVER THE YEARS the flower garden has been tamed and colour-coded and shaped into carefully laid out beds, and it is indeed foreign to our true landscape. And yet there is a link between these gardens and our cultural past. We should also consider their importance to our food systems and medicines, as well as the value their diversity carries. The exotics that were brought here on the first ships and those that have since trickled onto our shores have a cultural value as well as being supportive of our native fauna species.

There have, of course, been introduction disasters such as the rapid spread of invasive species like privet and gorse, although often their presence is more of an inconvenience to us than it is to nature. Even native plants are labelled pests in pastures, so it is important to differentiate between our habitat and the natural landscape. Vines such as morning glory, jasmine and old man's beard that wander into the bush and strangle trees are certainly a problem and we should not plant exotics that are likely to do harm to our fragile ecologies. But we now know better which are potential problem plants, and as long as our selections are educated and considered there is still a place for exotics in our urban gardens.

The production of food is, of course, one source of varied horticulture upon which we are dependent but there are other aspects to consider such as insects and bird life; for example, honey bees on which we depend not just for honey but also as a key pollinator for much of our food supply. Bees will do well in the bush on manuka or pohutukawa, among other native flowers, but to lure them into our gardens we need to have bee-attracting flowers on offer through the seasons.

First it is important to avoid flower species that may be aggressive and cause harm. They should also be avoided if to sustain them you need to constantly load your gardens with chemical cocktails. This is not

> The exotics that were brought here on the first ships and those that have since trickled onto our shores have a cultural value as well as being supportive of our native fauna species.

an approach that would have been favoured by Robinson, who studied the many aspects of a landscape and the different plants suited to each unique garden. While this rule may at first seem limiting, any experienced gardener will agree that limits are a relief. Such is the vastness and beauty of the plant world that choices can be overwhelming.

THIS, TOO, IS WHERE a colour scheme can be desirable, not just for the pleasure it gives the eye but also to help restrict the collector. Unlike a native or tropical garden, where we depend to a great extent on form and texture, a flower garden gives us an opportunity to play with colour. There's colour in foliage also, but colour in a flower garden offers the gardener the opportunity to be riotous.

The design of a flower garden is not just about sticking to simple colour schemes. It is also about conducting a year-round performance, with the blooms of one plant fading out as another's buds burst. A flower garden can, in fact, even change colour completely from the start of one season to the next. While this may seem like a challenging task, it need not be if you are happy to be patient and add to the palette through the seasons. This does require frequent trips to garden centres and specialty nurseries at all times of the year: plants are most alluring when in bloom and so regular trawling of the plant markets is likely to give you a constant effect.

This slow style of planning a garden gives you time to get to know your garden, discovering what grows best where and letting plants fill the spaces to which they are most suited. Don't write off a plant just because it doesn't do well in one spot. Persist, moving plants from place to place until you find their niche. Our garden environments are

> The design of a flower garden is not just about sticking to simple colour schemes. It is also about conducting a year-round performance, with the blooms of one plant fading out as another's buds burst.

generally more complex than we may first assume, and the discovery of this complexity contributes a good deal to the satisfaction of gardening. For example, in my Auckland garden it took four moves before I managed to grow Chatham Island forget-me-nots but the end result was well worth the initial failures.

You should also give some consideration to the depth of a garden bed if you want full effect. Thin rows make for constant work, and greatly limit your displays. For a splendid border four metres is advised, although in your average, shrinking, urban garden this is becoming less achievable. However, as a point of aspiration it might encourage you to be a bit more generous with the size of your garden beds in relation to the size of the lawn. While a grand lawn can be multi-purpose and suits most gardens, especially where children want open places to play, they do require high levels of maintenance and offer little diversity. One should never be afraid to give up lawn. I would suggest that a deep, beautiful flower border has more value than a lawn, especially on a front section where most people are unlikely to play or sit. There is plenty of pleasurable play for children in a garden that allows them to explore, climbing trees and hiding in shrubs and discovering the beauty and magic of flowers.

THERE IS A PERCEPTION, too, that a flower garden is a lot of work. However, it is possible to have flowers without spraying and fussing if you choose varieties that are well suited to your location and if you allow your garden to be soft and loose, balancing the blooms with structure and texture. There is also no reason that flowers and natives need to be seen as mutually exclusive. Instead, one can sell the other and these combinations can give your garden a look that is unique to your region.

In my own garden nothing delights me more than the uninvited occupation of cineraria that arrives every spring. They are now well established, and I carefully preserve them through the rest of the year because their splash of colour through a bank of green and stone is uplifting. It does not discriminate between the native ferns, trees

◄ **LEFT** This border at the Auckland
Botanic Gardens shows how deep
plantings allow for a spectacular show.
Blue echinops in the foreground brings
to life the yellows of kangaroo paws,
euphorbia and rudbeckias, while the deep
orange of the red ginger and canna punch
their way forward.

and shrubs towering around it. It is simply nature venturing into the cracks. This is the special joy of a wild garden, where we can allow plants to naturalise rather than constantly fighting to maintain rows and order.

It should be remembered, though, that while plants may be allowed to find their own form there still needs to be limits, and a wild garden is not an invitation for disregard. It is up to the gardener to ensure that some order is kept, especially close to buildings and paths. As the Australian landscape designer Edna Walling wrote, 'The garden should always be a bit bigger than you can keep tidy'. This is an attitude that I would encourage gardeners of all sorts to subscribe to.

Designer's guide

A FLOWER GARDEN colour scheme can be as broad or as limited as you want it to be. To include a broad range of colours, you can create transitions through the garden from one colour to the next so there is order in the informality. Complementary colours can be used to create transition. For example, you can move from a blue border into purples by grading the colours and dropping yellows in with the blues and oranges in with the purples. The orange tones then allow you to introduce crimsons, which may have been too severe next to a soft yellow. Allowing colour changes to drift through a garden gives you a visual journey, adding to the overall experience and creating a sense of discovery.

A flower garden is never about the flower colour alone. Colour should be looked for in stems and foliage, buds and even seed heads, the leaves on a tree and the flush of pink on the leaves of a fern. This requires close observation of the plants in your garden and the changes they undergo through different seasons. These changes may even mean that a border will transform with the seasons, and it is possible to have a garden that will change like a chameleon as the weather turns. This is

▶ **RIGHT** This simple colour scheme of purples and yellows includes statice, phlomis, hemerocallis and, far in the background, the yellow of kniphofia. All are hardy garden plants. Although this is a beautiful combination, the plants are competing for space, and another half-metre of depth in the border would make all the difference.

a master gardener's game but something to which all gardeners should aspire.

One of the great challenges of the flower garden is the constant change it is undergoing. While this transition is one of the joys, it can also result in unsightly holes in planting as flowers pass their peak. Selecting long-flowering species as well as species which have form, even in winter months, can help. So does blending flowers with evergreen plants such as grasses and divaricating shrubs to ensure year-round interest. The deeper your borders, the more opportunity you have to create layers. Adding evergreen shrubs also allows you to add a sculptural form to the garden, letting the eye rest and focus on a composition. Think of these solid forms as anchors in a haze of colour.

Like garden style, colour is very personal and everyone has a different preference. My best advice when choosing a colour scheme is to stay true to what you love. A gardener who follows his or her heart always has greater success than those who follow a trend. If you are a romantic, stay with soft gentle tones and smokey pastels. If you're vivacious let your garden be so too, and commit to strong tones that will hold up against each other. If you are somewhere in the middle, limit your colours, using one, two or three that will keep your garden cohesive.

CURVES

SOFT CURVING FORMS are a great way of increasing the illusion of depth in a smaller garden, allowing you to deepen beds in places while maximising open spaces where they are required. It also provides opportunities to form nooks and intimate spaces. We all like to be able to nestle into a corner when we are seeking quiet time, especially on a sunny afternoon with a good book.

While curves work well for borders, it is not necessary to go overboard. Functional spaces such as decks and service areas should be designed to be efficient. Wildness in a garden should not come at the

◄ **LEFT** Echinacea is one of Piet Oudolf's signature plants. The secret to growing it well is gravelly beds with little watering and not too much compost. Hot sun is an absolute must. Not only is echinacea an attractive plant, it is also wonderful for attracting pollinators.

expense of efficiency, in fact quite the opposite. Strong, simple paving forms relate to architecture, and when designing areas closer to the house that have frequent usage, I am always inclined to maintain the simplicity of the form. This strong use of form provides a contrast to the softness of drifty, naturalistic plantings.

GROUPINGS AND LAYOUT

IT'S LONG BEEN a rule of garden design that one should plant in odd numbers, and I would have to agree with this especially if the effect you wish to create is informal and wild. Informal, however, doesn't mean there is not an order or rules to follow. Even nature works in sweeps of plants, with detail around the cracks and crevices on the edges and in layers. Planting should always start from the top down, with consideration being given first to the position of trees and hedges. These vertical planes are incredibly important in a garden, filling a large part of the mass of a garden space and affecting significantly what can grow beneath and in the surrounding areas.

This is one advantage of a flower garden, as it lends itself to deciduous trees that can offer windows of winter sun yet provide welcome shade in the summer months. Once these elements have been placed then you add another layer of structure with evergreen shrubs and grasses that give you depth and pivot points to swing sweeps of perennials around. Stone, too, can be introduced at this stage as well as other garden structures such as pieces of art that you want your planting to frame.

Once you have laid out a grouping of plants, consider pulling one or two plants away from the main group. This does a couple of things. First, it creates a more natural look, as if seeds had fallen in a cluster, with the odd one bouncing away or being dragged further by the wind. It is also a good way to link colours and plants, rather than making an abrupt change. This mimicry of nature is the key to creating a wild garden that still has order and reason.

Repetition in planting does not need to be formal and instead can mimic nature in sweeping brushstrokes.

▼ **BELOW AND RIGHT** At the end of a season most plants can do with being cut back, but at their peak let them fight it out and mingle. As long as your spacings are correct, plants will do well with a little competition and the effect of a garden that's full and overflowing is most pleasing. Here at Dalton's Plantation gardens, *Gaura* 'Whirling Butterflies' mingles with tall cleome, marigolds and echinacea. Open-flowered species of roses are more attractive to bees than modern hybrids.

► **RIGHT** New Zealand natives give us plenty of opportunity to experiment with new combinations. Here *Astelia* 'Silver Spear' and *Ligularia reniformis*, with its green dish-like leaves, provide form among drifts of flowers. Soft purple scabiosa in the foreground links with lavender, while rudbeckias add some bright yellow to the mix.

▼ **FOLLOWING PAGES** This outstanding display of helenium at the Auckland Botanic Gardens is a wonderful example of a flower garden that is neither blousy nor understated. Helenium flower well into late autumn, when much of the summer colour is starting to fade.

If you are following a planting plan, use it as you would a guide rather than as a strict set of rules. What appears to work on paper may not be possible on your site, where the land may slope, or where there's an ugly view of a neighbouring garage roof that you may want to block but that hasn't been considered in the plan. Check your placement as you go and use your knowledge of individual plants to make changes. The plants you lay out will be fresh from the garden centre and fairly small, so you need to grow them in your mind as you lay the garden out, thinking of their form as they grow and of their finished height. Height is of great importance in a perennial border where the variation in size between different plants may not be very great, and it is important that you know which should be furthest forward.

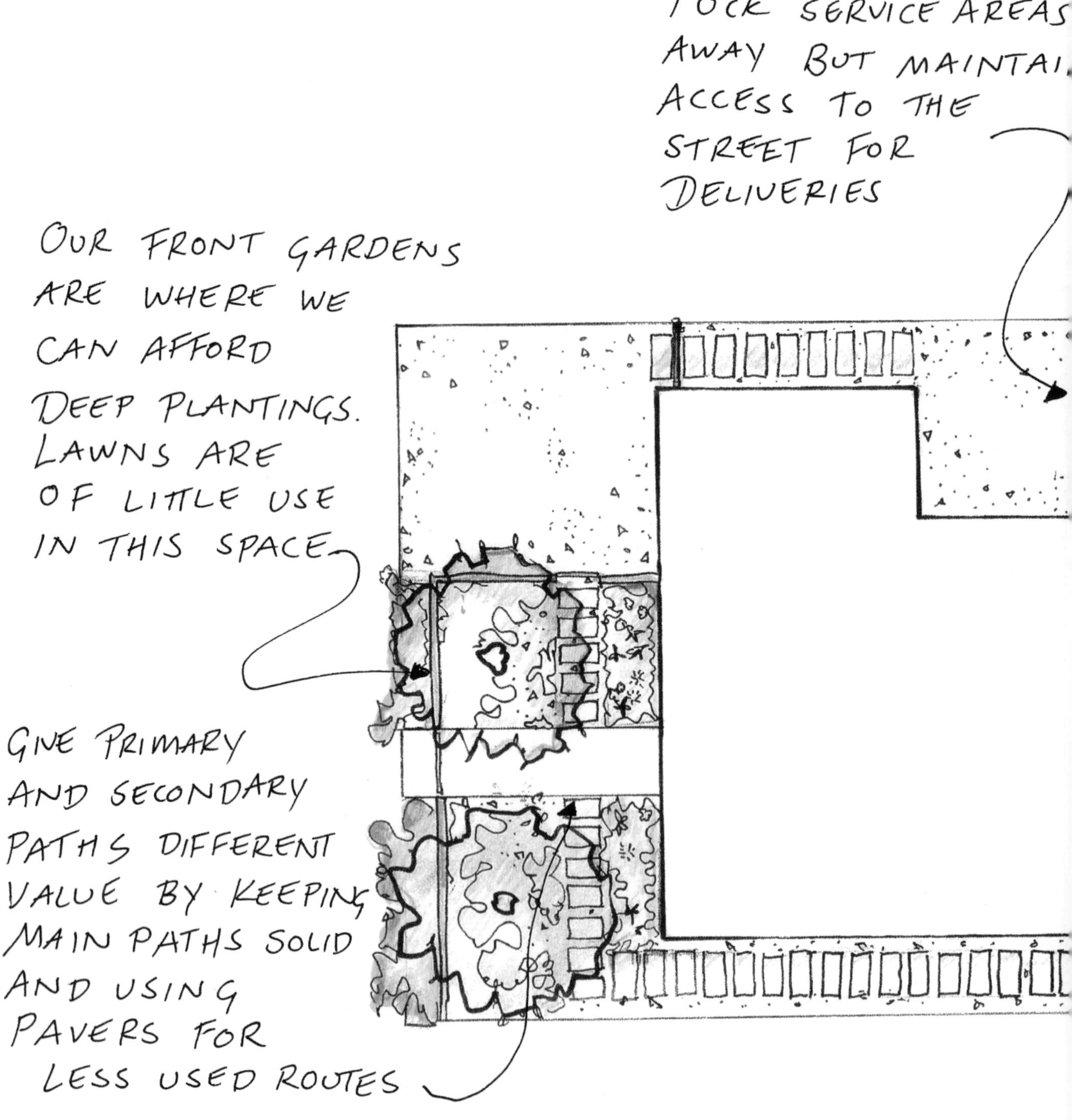

TUCK SERVICE AREAS
AWAY BUT MAINTAI[N]
ACCESS TO THE
STREET FOR
DELIVERIES

OUR FRONT GARDENS
ARE WHERE WE
CAN AFFORD
DEEP PLANTINGS.
LAWNS ARE
OF LITTLE USE
IN THIS SPACE.

GIVE PRIMARY
AND SECONDARY
PATHS DIFFERENT
VALUE BY KEEPING
MAIN PATHS SOLID
AND USING
PAVERS FOR
LESS USED ROUTES

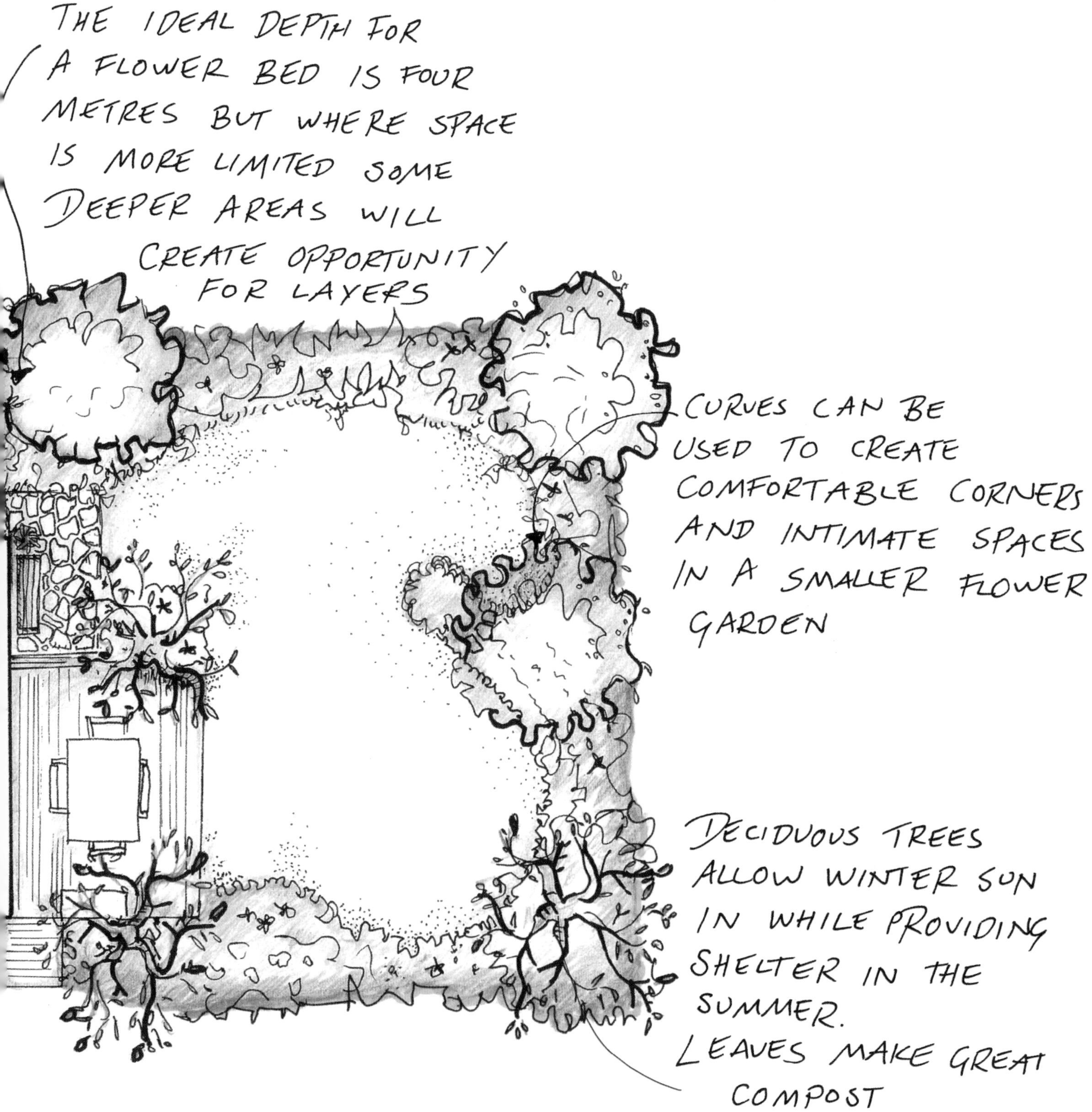

THE IDEAL DEPTH FOR
A FLOWER BED IS FOUR
METRES BUT WHERE SPACE
IS MORE LIMITED SOME
DEEPER AREAS WILL
CREATE OPPORTUNITY
FOR LAYERS

CURVES CAN BE
USED TO CREATE
COMFORTABLE CORNERS
AND INTIMATE SPACES
IN A SMALLER FLOWER
GARDEN

DECIDUOUS TREES
ALLOW WINTER SUN
IN WHILE PROVIDING
SHELTER IN THE
SUMMER.
LEAVES MAKE GREAT
COMPOST

PLANT GUIDE

Salvia spp.
SALVIA
A large family of perennials which includes many medicinal plants. Worth investigating for colours, hardiness and aromatic leaves.

Hylotelephium telephium
AUTUMN SEDUM
This perennial brings colour and form to the garden in late autumn, when little else is up and about. Also a great plant for bees at this time of year.

Pelargonium spp.
GERANIUM
A wonderful plant to swap with friends. Particularly delightful clambering through or against a fence.

Helenium spp.
HELENIUM
This perennial is divine mixed with a grass such as anemanthele, particularly when autumn tones come to the garden.

Iris spp.
IRIS
A huge family of plants without which no flower garden is complete. Suit a wide range of conditions from dry and free draining to pond side. Most like full sun.

Dahlia spp.
DAHLIA
You will normally purchase dahlias as tubers from late June. Always popular in perennial borders, expect this plant to be noticed when it's in action.

Rudbeckia spp.
RUDBECKIA
This late-summer and autumn colour is ideal for deep borders where you are looking to create a year-round effect.

Achillea spp.
ACHILLEA
Coming in a range of vibrant colours, this hardy perennial is beautiful in textural plantings with divaricates and grasses.

Argyranthemum frutescens
MARGUERITE DAISY
This family of daisies offer a broad colour palette and are easy-care cheerful garden plants.

Stachys byzantina
LAMB'S EARS

This fluffy leaved plant looks, as its name suggests, like lambs' ears. Also carries purple flowers in spring.

Papaver spp.
POPPY

I always make room in my small flower border for poppies. Can be grown from seed for a good choice of colours; plants are available in spring and summer.

Rosa spp.
ROSE

Must be the poster girl for a flower garden. It's important to find varieties that perform well in your region. Botanic gardens are a great reference point.

Lavandula spp.
LAVENDER

Another great plant for bees. Extremely aromatic and can be used to freshen drawers and in pillows to aid sleep (as long as you don't have a sensitive nose!).

Delphinium spp.
DELPHINIUM

A treat for Christmas and into late-summer. The towering flower heads are worth the wait. Can be prone to powdery mildew.

Penstemon spp.
PENSTEMON

A great plant for pinks and purples near the front of a border. Growing around 400–600 flower heads, it will continue to flower if regularly pruned back.

Echinacea spp.
CONE FLOWER

Cones should be left on after flowering so seed will distribute, and so you can enjoy them on a dewy or frosty winter morning.

Lilium spp.
LILY

Popular as a cut flower but I think they are best grown in a garden where the scent can drift and the pollen can fall as intended.

Miscanthus sinensis
MISCANTHUS

A two-metre high grass, dramatic from its tall stripy foliage, to its wispy flowers, until it becomes dry and dormant.

Heliotropium arborescens
CHERRY PIE
This perennial is well worth growing en masse. The scent is absolutely heavenly and flowers consistent through most summer months. Needs good drainage.

Alstroemeria spp.
ALSTROEMERIA
A very reliable garden plant that will flower freely even in partial shade. Mixes beautifully with grasses. Heights range from 300mm to a metre high.

Gaura spp.
WHIRLING BUTTERFLIES
A great perennial when used in combination with grasses. The delicate flowers repeat through late spring and summer and into autumn.

Anemanthele lessoniana
GOSSAMER GRASS
Beautiful with flowers, the drooping form is both graceful and tidy. The seed heads are an added pleasure in the spring garden.

Liriope muscari
LIRIOPE
An excellent deep-green, thick-leaved groundcover with the added joy of a carpet of flowers in late summer. Watch the snails though.

Euphorbia spp.
EUPHORBIA
A great plant for texture and form. Euphorbias vary in colour but tend to share the characteristic yellow green blooms.

Canna spp.
CANNA
Often taken for granted, this versatile perennial is great for the back of borders. Prune back any scruffy-looking flowers or foliage and they will continue to perform.

Thamnochortus cinereus
RESTIO
These hardy reeds are a wonderful addition where a contemporary look is desired. The seed heads add a hazy texture to the garden.

Hydrangea macrophylla
HYDRANGEA
Colours will change depending on the pH of your soil and the season. Pink is acid, blue is neutral and plum is normally the start of autumn.

Ligularia 'Britt Marie Crawford'
LIGULARIA
With wonderful foliage and flowers that are a very bright yellow and either loved or hated. If you don't like, just deadhead before they open.

SHADE

Myosotis spp.
FORGET-ME-NOT
Great to sow in difficult shady areas beneath trees and shrubs. Though an annual, will self-sow once established so long as you don't accidentally weed them out.

Hosta spp.
HOSTA
This shade-loving perennial has attractive blue and white flowers but its foliage is just as much, if not more, of a feature as long as you can keep the snails away!

Prunus spp.
CHERRY TREE
Though the flowers may be short-lived they are such a mark of the change of season that they're worth your patience. Blossom is best in cool gardens.

Helleborus spp.
WINTER ROSE
As the name suggests this is the ideal winter flower and also grows comfortably in woodland conditions alongside ferns.

Anemone hybrida cultivar
JAPANESE ANEMONE
Ideal for dry, difficult shade. Though the foliage is not much to look at it covers the ground well and the autumn flowers are a bright delight.

OTHER PLANTS TO CONSIDER

SUN

Corokia spp.
COROKIA

Convolvulus cneorum
SILVER BUSH

Armeria spp.
THRIFT

Sisyrinchium striatum
SATIN FLOWER

Allium spp.
GARLIC, ONION, CHIVES

Crocosmia spp.
CROCOSMIA 'LUCIFER'

Kniphofia spp.
RED HOT POKER

SUN-SHADE

Rosmarinus spp.
ROSEMARY

Erysimum spp.
WALLFLOWER

Convolvulus mauritanicus
GROUND MORNING GLORY

Acer spp.
MAPLE

SHADE

Clivia spp.
CLIVIA

Astelia spp.
ASTELIA

THE NATURAL
Subtropical
Garden

In warmer climates with high rainfall, garden seasonality is replaced by an intensity of green that is so constant we can forgive the lack of drama that punctuates the turning of the seasons in other garden situations.

This is the sort of garden that gives the gardener the opportunity to explore all the shades of green, and where foliage, form and texture dominate. But colour and flowers should not be abandoned altogether; rather, a lush green backdrop allows us to embrace the bold colours that may look garish in subtler settings. It is the sort of garden in which deep reds and oranges and even hot pinks sing. Wildness comes naturally to the subtropical garden, where the speed of growth makes exerting discipline a challenge. I grew up in this climate, and so the subtropical garden was one of the first styles I really embraced.

▲ **PREVIOUS PAGES** The curving fronds of palms and bananas here invite us into a tropical paradise. Nothing evokes intrigue more than a drive that disappears before it reveals its destination. The mass planting of bromeliads is most suited to this situation where the movement is long and simple.

Colour combinations should not be limited to flowers or even foliage. Even the stems of a plant can add to a theme, as the orange of this ornamental banana does with the hot flowers of leonotis in the foreground.

► **RIGHT** There is nothing quite as appealing as beautiful stepping stones floating through natural plantings. These are over a shallow pond planted with lotus and iris and create a point of focus as well as an attractive path.

WHETHER NATIVE OR EXOTIC, the plants that inhabit the subtropical garden are leafy and tend to range from grass-green into rich blue-based greens and even blacks. The size of the leaf is the main indicator of its ideal growing conditions: only where both warmth and wet combine can a plant afford to grow thick dish-like leaves.

The intensity of green is also a reflection of lush growing conditions. And if there is one garden style in which using water as a focus makes sense then it's the subtropical. The rich foliage signals an abundant supply of water. In the absence of a water feature such as a rill or pond, groundcovers running through rocks can imitate the natural flow of a stream. They also create space and focus in a planting composition, leading the eye onward through otherwise dense plantings. Space is an important design aspect in the subtropical garden, and it allows us to create layers of planting without the garden becoming overcrowded and unruly. In other words, jungle.

Large volcanic stones can be used against the large leaves and will be quickly dwarfed by the foliage, so use them boldly. They should be placed not only to create layers through natural curves but so they also become part of the function of the garden, forming seats and stepping stones through beds. There is nothing like the warmth of a sun-kissed stone to sit on after a day in the garden.

Wherever possible, the goal is to create multiple layers of green. The gardener should look not only to his or her own garden but also beyond, to attractive trees and foliage in neighbouring properties; using these 'borrowed' landscapes in your design adds depth to views.

Rather than marking the boundary with an expensive wall medium, shrubs can blend in with external features that can then be drawn in with deeper layers of planting. This allows you to create the appearance of deep beds that are then thinned out to open up areas for lawn or paved areas.

ONE OF THE great strengths of the subtropical garden is the tall slender form of many palm trees. They will, in time, reach towering

◄ **LEFT** This is a good example of native plants integrated into a tropical planting. The groundcover muehlenbeckia creates space that emphasises the form of both the palms, specimen cordyline and the silver leaves of the cussonia. The plantings are highlighted with a drift of bright red blood grass.

heights but they are not as broad as many other trees, making them perfect for narrow urban spaces. Issues of height can be managed with generational plantings, where palms are planted at different stages of maturity, providing foliage at different heights as they grow. As the mature specimens outgrow a site, there is a second generation coming through and a new generation can be planted. This rotational planting is a valid response in a city environment, where large specimens may impose on sunlight. It is better than not planting, or removing trees altogether, and as long as the organic material is put to good use or composted on-site it has few drawbacks. After all, this is how forests and much of nature work, with only the strongest or most well-sited specimens reaching great ages.

One of the great strengths of the subtropical garden is the tall slender form of many palm trees.

When planting palms, consideration should be given to how invasive they may be. You should seek out local advice on invasive varieties before selecting species — displays of berries are one of the fine features of many palm species, making them very attractive to birds and rodents who happily spread the seeds far and wide. If you are concerned about ecology, our native nikau palm is a fine specimen and one we welcome birds spreading.

WHILE SUBTROPICAL GARDENS can be filled with enticing exotics, many of our natives have similar attributes that can be used to similar dramatic effect. It's the large glossy leaves that make these plants so appealing: puka, kapuka, kawakawa and coprosma all have the sheen required. The kaka beak is also a wonderful garden plant for hot colour, with outstanding flowers that must be breathtaking to come across in the bush; a pleasure few of us have as this is an endangered plant in the wild.

A subtropical garden also offers a wonderful opportunity to celebrate the unique flora of the Pacific region with hibiscus and frangipani, should you live in a warm enough part of the country to be able to grow these more frost-tender favourites. While locality can limit what we grow, it also allows us to celebrate regionalism and help guide us into creating gardens that have a unique flavour, engaging the natural environment and local cultural history with our own style. On my boundary there's a banana planted by a previous Samoan neighbour that I'm lucky to be able to share. It has proven extremely hardy to Auckland's climate and it produces the sweetest small bananas that are greatly enjoyed by our children. Taro, too, is easily grown as are pawpaw and loquats. Even citrus will sit attractively in amongst lush foliage, and passionfruit, if you can keep the passion vine hoppers away, will offer splendid blooms as well as fruit up against a hot fence.

COLOUR IS of course an important part of Pacific culture, and in the subtropical garden it can be abundant and bold. Washed-out colours are likely to disappear, while deep bright blooms glow out from the tangling layers. Skilled and creative gardeners throw colour into other aspects of the garden; hot-coloured walls or tiled mosaics, for example, can be used to great effect. Colour can also be utilised in garden furniture such as hammocks or outdoor beanbags that help transform your garden into a place for a holiday at home.

Colour is of course an important part of Pacific culture and in the subtropical garden it can be abundant and bold.

There is no doubt that layers of lush green are good for our well-being. Research has indicated that the ideal garden for well-being is 70 per cent greenscaping and 30 per cent hard surfaces. Even in a small space, lush layers of tropical foliage can grant you this effect.

Design guide

THE BEST ADVICE I can give someone wanting to create a foliage garden is to embrace the groundcover. Low, densely matting plants not only allow us to eliminate bare unsightly soil but they also create breadth in a garden. It is easy for a garden to become overcrowded, and sweeps of low-lying groundcovers help us to keep open spaces that allow us to view the forms and textures of the surrounding plants.

Texture and form are most important, and in most cases this should be planned for before consideration is given to colour. Be careful not to become too repetitive with shapes and think about the contrasts between different types of leaves. It is easy to tend towards large glossy leaves and forget about the finer textures that provide the contrast.

Grasses, reeds and ferns should be on the list, even if they are used as details in cracks and crevices. Nothing makes a garden feel more complete and alive than plants that appear as if they may have snuck in after the master plan. The base of a rock provides a perfect opportunity for this. In nature, water pools and creeps around rock, making this a place where a fern or herbaceous plant may be able to prosper and find shelter. Depending on their colour and type, rocks also reflect or absorb warmth, creating very specific growing conditions in their immediate vicinity and allowing you, if you choose, to sneak a special specimen into the mix.

COLOUR

IT IS GENERALLY accepted that bright colour is appropriate for a tropical garden and it's easy to see why. The rich lush layers of green need a confident response and soft tones can easily be lost. Blues and purples are also more difficult to use in a palette of green, and can send the wrong message. These colours associate more pleasantly with a warm but dry garden. Reds, oranges and yellows, on the other hand, while not at all

◄ **LEFT** This is a good example of a mature tropical planting and of the scale of plants. The reds of the bromeliad provide plenty of colour, which could be picked up with red flowers like *Lobelia* 'Queen Victoria' and black cannas. Here, however, it is highlighted with the orange of strelitzia (bird of paradise) and epidendrum.

out of place in a dry garden, signal a warmth and richness that marries well with the decadence of a tropical garden. This is not to say that a subtropical garden is ostentatious but it does require warmth and wet.

Nor should colour be fussy; instead it should be bold, be it in the size of the flowers or the simplicity of the sweeps of mass planting. Cannas, hibiscus, blood lilies and abutilon will inject seasonal shots of colour into a lush backdrop while otherwise blending into the background.

SCENT

IF WE ARE talking decadence then you might as well hit all the senses and ensure our noses are not neglected. Although their flowers may not be bold, a daphne or gardenia hidden in the foliage delivers such reliable scent that they deserve to be considered. They are both often labelled as difficult to grow but I think placement and fertiliser are the key to success. Both plants do best sitting north-west or north-east and neither in the shade nor the sun but rather skirting the edge of an overhang so they are kissed by sun and rain but not drowned in either. They are also hungry plants, liking monthly applications of sheep pellets and Epsom salts in spring, summer and autumn. Get these details right and they are trouble-free plants with foliage that can be convincingly worked into any tropical garden.

CHILDREN AND STONE

PARENTS OFTEN REQUEST a flat lawn for children, but there is nothing more inviting to a child than a garden with twists and turns that can engage their imagination. Large boulders sitting in a subtropical bed not only form seats but can also become a herd of elephants, the turret of a castle, or islands in an ocean swarming with poisonous jellyfish and giant squid. Stepping stones through groundcover can allow free flow through the garden, making it engaging. Rather than the garden being out of bounds, children can be encouraged to appreciate its form and respect it for the right reasons. The loss of the occasional precious plant is of course to be expected, but a small price to pay for offspring who one day will surprise you and themselves with an interest in gardening whose seed was sown in their childhood.

WATER

THE ABILITY TO CAPTURE and contain a fresh supply of water has long been an essential aspect of landscape design, long before water could be accessed so readily. You may decide to build a water feature in your subtropical garden, but even if you don't, you should still imagine where water might flow beneath the soil as you plan your garden layout. Expressing the source of water in a garden is an abstract tool that creates a magic that's hard to define. Look at the form of your site and think of the path that water would take through it, and use this to form valleys of green and to create shapes within your planting. Look at waterfalls, streams, rivers and estuaries and take inspiration from these patterns, applying them to your garden as if you are revealing an underwater stream. Frame it with darker colours and deep reds, but let the 'water' be a calming green pool or path through the composition.

> Expressing the source of water in a garden is an abstract tool that creates a magic that's hard to define.

If you wish to use a real water feature you need to decide whether it is to be part of the natural form of the garden or part of the architecture. There is nothing more uncomfortable than a water feature sitting somewhere in between. To be natural it must make sense within the overall pattern of the garden. Water always flows downward, and has a path, so if the position of a 'naturalistic' water feature opposes reason it is always less convincing and is more inclined to look like an aquarium.

◂ **LEFT** This water feature in photographer Gil Hanly's garden is a nice example of how art can reinforce the narrative in a garden. These ceramic ducks look ready to launch themselves into the water.

Of course, if you are wanting to invest in a water feature you need it to be a point of focus in a garden, and sometimes this may not make sense in the arrangement of the landscape. In this case you are best to separate it from the natural form of the garden and instead transport and contain the water using crisp and deliberate lines that make sense of its movement and allow it to be moved around against gravity.

Sound is also an important aspect of water and should be carefully considered in the design. Large torrents can be distracting, while a slow constant drip has been used as a form of torture. Somewhere in between is delightful: a babble or gurgle or soft splash. You need to think about a balance between the sound of the water and the sight of water movement which, spread over a large surface, will capture changes in light and reflection, allowing the mood of the garden to alter through the day. Moving water slowly over a large surface is very effective although it does take a lot of force, so make sure you have researched pumps adequately to ensure the effect will match your expectations.

SPLASH ALSO NEEDS to be considered, and the greater the fall of water the more likely you will be faced with challenges, especially if you want to create friction with a textured surface. If you have too much texture, such as protruding pebbles, the water feature will need a large catchment beneath to catch the spray. A small amount, on the other hand, will help the water cling to the surface.

You also need to consider how you deal with the point at which the water spills. Pipe size not only affects the flow but the pipes themselves can be unsightly and need to be masked in the design. This is especially the case with natural water features that should show nothing of the mechanism that drives the water. The aspiration should be to create the illusion that the water has a natural source and point of departure.

One of the greatest challenges is to contain the water. Concrete ponds, especially in organic forms, are very prone to cracking and therefore leaking, and once a leak establishes it is both hard to find and

challenging to repair. Plastic liners are by far the most reliable form of water retention but they need to be hidden by pebbles or other stone, and this can be quite challenging when trying to create a natural effect.

Earth ponds are certainly the most beautiful: they allow you to plant into the margins and so the transition from water to garden can be as seamless or continuous as you desire. A liner can also be moulded to create planting shelves and pockets so that the transition appears continuous. If you can find stones large enough to overhang in places, this can also help the overall effect.

Generally I would advise against using still water in a garden; the problems caused by stagnant water are many. Exceptions, however, are what make great design and in this case the lotus is a great ally. Lotus require shallow, still water and are the perfect plant for a subtropical garden, both for their absolute beauty and for the spiritual significance they have for many cultures. If space is restricted, a simple bowl is enough to bring both water and this special plant into a garden.

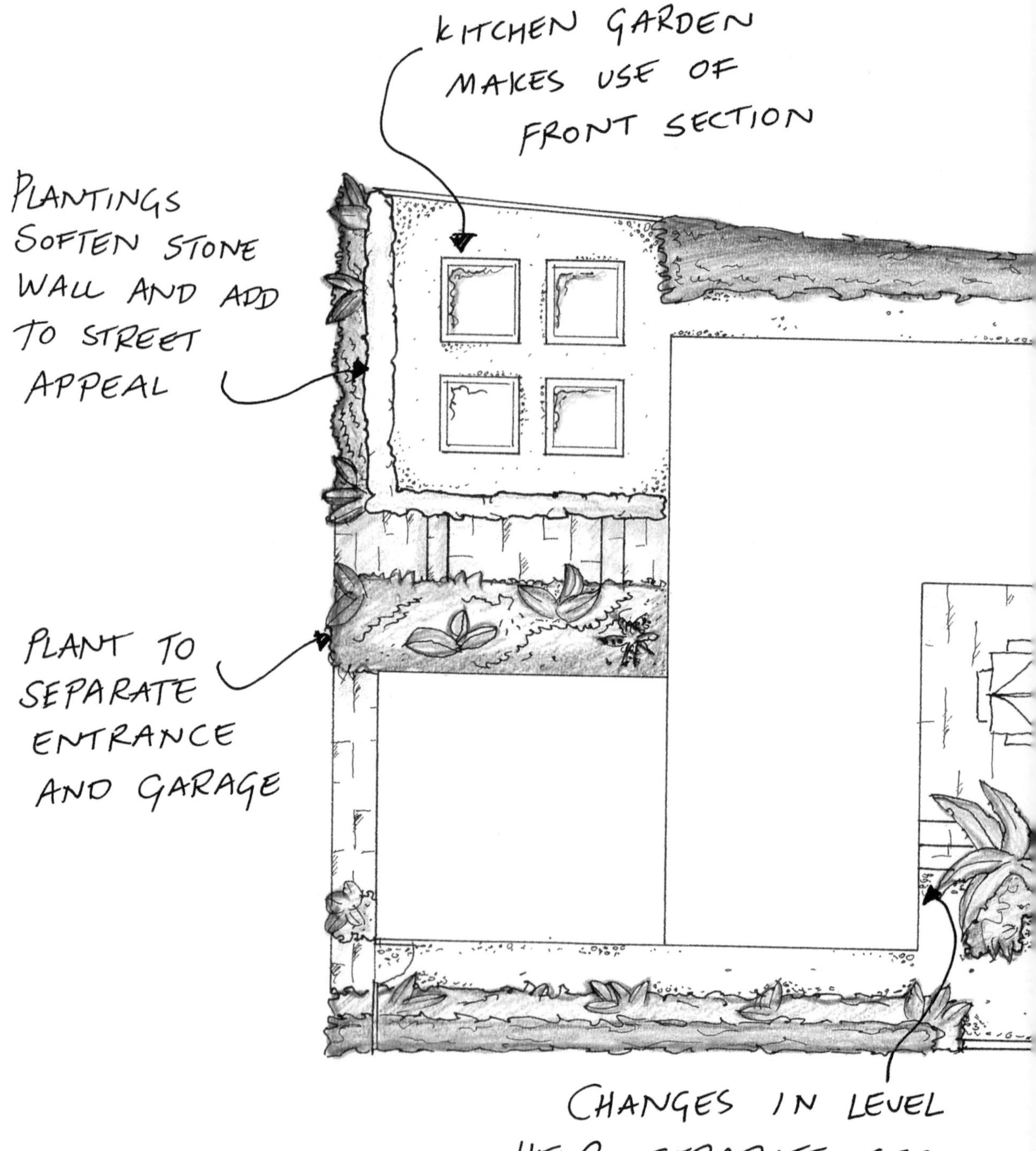

KITCHEN GARDEN
MAKES USE OF
FRONT SECTION

PLANTINGS
SOFTEN STONE
WALL AND ADD
TO STREET
APPEAL

PLANT TO
SEPARATE
ENTRANCE
AND GARAGE

CHANGES IN LEVEL
HELP SEPARATE SPACES

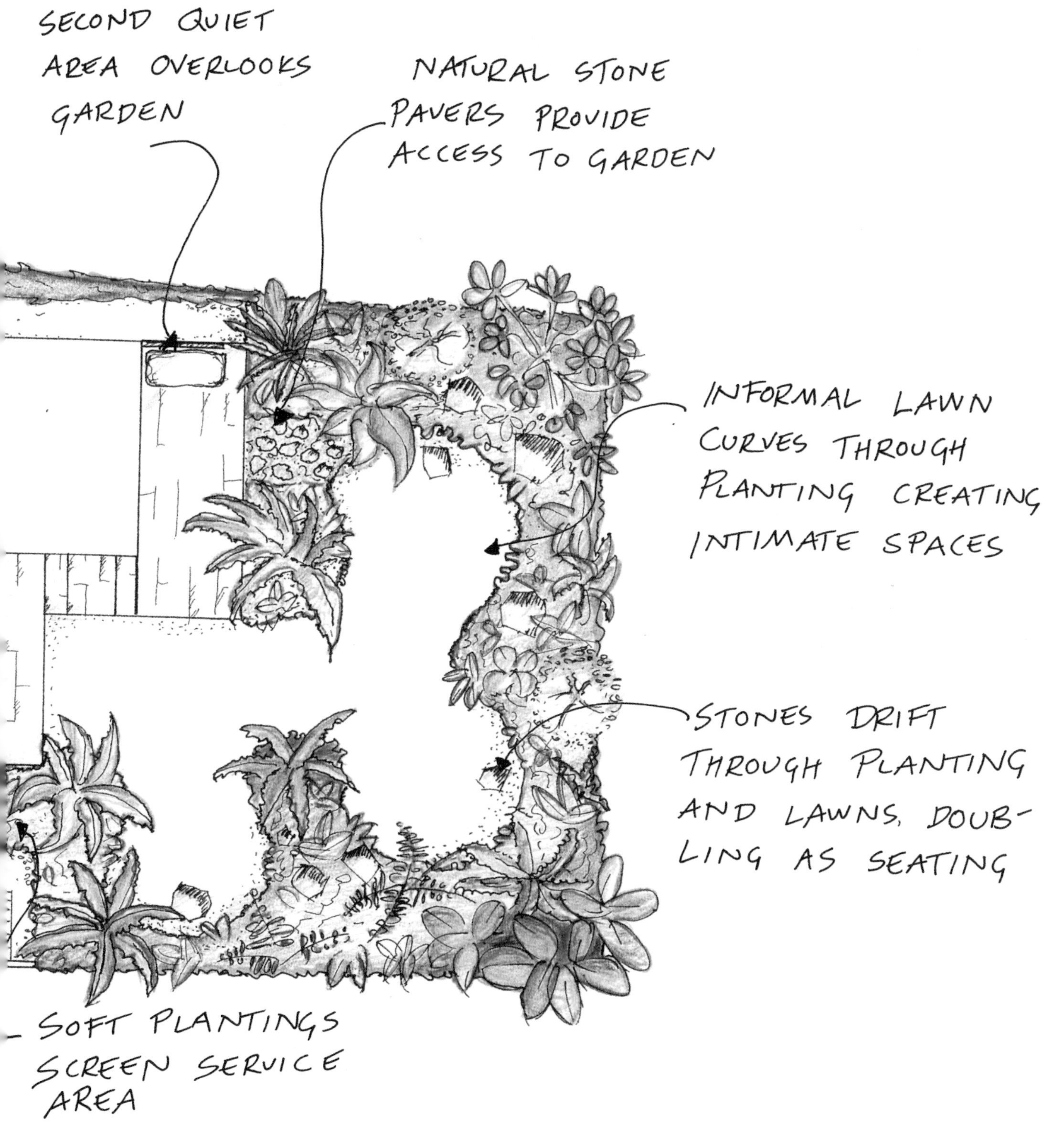

SECOND QUIET
AREA OVERLOOKS
GARDEN

NATURAL STONE
PAVERS PROVIDE
ACCESS TO GARDEN

INFORMAL LAWN
CURVES THROUGH
PLANTING CREATING
INTIMATE SPACES

STONES DRIFT
THROUGH PLANTING
AND LAWNS, DOUB-
LING AS SEATING

SOFT PLANTINGS
SCREEN SERVICE
AREA

PALMS

Musa spp.
BANANA

For best foliage, plant ornamental varieties which are short-lived. Fruiting varieties have scrappier foliage but if pruned back annually stay looking good.

Howea forsteriana
KENTIA

An excellent slow-growing palm that holds its form and is less inclined to get tatty leaves. Also not as invasive as some other garden palms.

Rhopalostylis sapida
NIKAU

Our only native palm. Large specimens are expensive so plant young palms beneath others. With time you will get beautiful plants.

SHRUBS AND TREES

Pseudopanax lessonii
HOUPARA

This slender shrub is an excellent option where screening is required. Great in shade as well as sun and has well-defined leaves.

Griselinia spp.
KAPUKA

Both *G. littoralis* and *G. lucida* (larger leaf) are excellent hedging plants in a foliage garden. Needs free-draining soil and will grow in sun and semi-shade.

Brugmansia spp.
DATURA

An amazing tree with dramatic flowers. Be aware, though, that it is poisonous if consumed.

Schefflera spp.
UMBRELLA TREE

Has an attractive open form which makes it a great tall tree for year-round screening with dappled light.

Meryta sinclairii
PUKA

A great specimen for a foliage garden. When it outgrows a space, prune it back to several branches and it will bush out even more with fresh heads.

Cussonia spp.
CUSSONIA

Simply outstanding for an absolutely unique form. Wonderful as a specimen in the garden or a large container.

Hibiscus spp.
HIBISCUS

Needing little introduction, an obvious addition to any tropical garden. The secret is to prune every spring to maintain dense form.

Plumeria spp.
FRANGIPANI

Great for a patio or verandah. Can be grown in a sheltered north-facing garden with volcanic soil or in planters as a feature. Lovely evening fragrance.

Daphne odora
DAPHNE

Though old-fashioned, daphne has a scent that suits the character of a tropical garden. Grows well in the dappled light beneath palms.

GROUNDCOVER, FORM AND TEXTURE

Ligularia reniformis
TRACTOR SEAT

Artist Friedensreich Hundertwasser grew this on the houseboat he sailed from Austria to New Zealand. A reliable plant unrivalled for its circular leaf form.

Acorus gramineus
SLENDER SWEET FLAG

Popular in Japanese gardens, this elegant soft-leafed grass grows in swirls and adds wonderful texture and highlight to a shady corner.

Colocasia esculenta
TARO

A terrific addition to a garden where large leafy form is required. Be aware they are vigorous and need to be well maintained.

Ajuga reptans 'Jungle Beauty'
AJUGA

A wonderfully leafy groundcover. Very reliable in shade and sun with consistent water supply. Purple flowers in summer are an added bonus.

Lobelia angulata
PANAKENAKE

Recently renamed (was *Pratia angulata*). This groundcover grows best with plenty of water and sun. A carpet of white when flowering.

Asplenium bulbiferum
HEN AND CHICKEN FERN

One of the most popular landscape ferns and with good reason. A very reliable garden plant that introduces a lovely soft texture to the foliage garden.

Canna spp.
CANNA
Not only great for flower colour but the foliage also comes in hot colours and is lush and leafy. Includes a newly released black canna.

Imperata cylindrica
BLOOD GRASS
This deciduous grass is a brilliantly coloured texture to introduce to a foliage garden. Great grown through groundcover.

Lobelia cardinalis 'Queen Victoria'
LOBELIA 'QUEEN VICTORIA'
These water-loving perennials provide a wonderful injection of colour that's hard to beat in a tropical garden.

Selliera radicans
REMUREMU
A hardy groundcover and an excellent lawn alternative, carpeted in white flowers over summer. Weeds can be controlled by occasional doses of sea water.

Bromeliad neoregelia
BROMELIAD
Bromeliads are a favourite in tropical gardens but less is more. Their form can be lost if overplanted. Thin as they pup to keep at their best.

Lobelia aberdarica
GIANT LOBELIA
Likes free-draining soil with a good water supply. Amazing soft rosettes of foliage bear blue spires when mature.

Scadoxus spp.
SCADOXUS
It's not often that you can get this degree of colour in dry shade — this perennial is the exception to the rule.

Hemerocallis spp.
DAYLILY
While the foliage is not particularly impressive, this is a hardy and reliable perennial that comes in a vast range of colours to suit most tastes.

Strelitzia spp.
BIRD OF PARADISE
A wonderful alternative to a traditional hedge in a tropical garden, with the added benefit of no trimming. *S. juncea* has the most elegant form.

Cycas revoluta
CYCAD
A garden classic and one of the most ancient plants alive today. Though slow-growing, they are highly sought-after for their excellent form and reliability.

Soleirolia soleirolii
BABY'S TEARS
This is a vigorous cover for moist shade. Fresh green moss-like effect.

Ficus dammaropsis
FICUS
This spectacular large-leafed tree is glorious. Hard to track down —
a collector's treat.

OTHER PLANTS TO CONSIDER

PALMS

Phoenix roebelenii
MINIATURE DATE PALM

Dypsis lutescens
CANE PALM

Caryota mitis
FISHTAIL PALM

Adonidia merrillii
MANILA PALM

Monstera deliciosa
FRUIT SALAD PLANT

SHRUBS AND GROUNDCOVER

Abutilon spp.
LANTERN FLOWER

Heliconia spp.
LOBSTER CLAW

Rhododendron spp.
VIREYA RHODODENDRON

Albizia julibrissin
SILK TREE

Cussonia paniculata
MOUNTAIN CABBAGE TREE

Stenocarpus sinuatus
FIREWHEEL TREE

Gardenia 'Professor Pucci'
GARDENIA

PERENNIALS AND GROUNDCOVER

Muehlenbeckia axillaris
CREEPING POHUEHUE

Hippeastrum spp.
AMARYLLIS

Trachelospermum jasminoides
STAR JASMINE

FORM AND TEXTURE

Vriesea hieroglyphica
KING OF THE BROMELIADS

Cyathea medullaris
MAMAKU

Xanthorrhoea australis
GRASS TREE

Philodendron 'Xanadu'
XANADU

Lomandra 'Tanika'
LOMANDRA

Bergenia cordifolia
BERGENIA

THE NATURAL
Productive
Garden

Growing food is as simple as it is complicated. The main challenge that most people face is the commitment of time. But then think of the hours spent in supermarket queues and driving back and forth in traffic. The more food we can grow ourselves, the more we can liberate ourselves from the less enjoyable shackles of modernity. The pleasure of growing your own fresh food is not just in the satisfaction of growing but also in the flavour, the colour and the quirky forms of home-grown produce that are unmatched by the regular shapes of commercially grown crops.

▲ **PREVIOUS PAGE** Growing beans on a double-sided triangular frame is an efficient way to double your crop. When the plants are small you can grow greens such as spinach and herbs beneath; then, as the beans shade them out, you can sow nasturtium, which is a great companion plant tolerant of shade.

▶ **RIGHT** A simple garden by Queenstown landscape architect Ralf Krüger.

MORE THAN ANY other garden, the design of a productive garden needs to be led by function. Whatever your situation, you need to be realistic about what you can manage in terms of production, maintenance and harvest. It is also important to plan a garden that is suited to your physical abilities. If you have back problems then raised beds are ideal. And remember, don't take on too much as a productive garden quickly loses its joy if it becomes overwhelming. Just because you start small doesn't mean you can't have grand plans for the future.

For most people a modest vegetable patch and a few favoured fruit trees are more than enough to satisfy. But for the enthusiast who wants a wide range of fresh food free from chemicals and full of nutrition, a more complex growing system is ideal. Complex, however, doesn't mean more work; it just means rich in diversity — not just for the garden but also for your diet, which is surely an ideal way to live.

> There is no doubt that food production has a different aesthetic than other gardening styles but all the same it is not without beauty, reason or order.

The main challenge, though, in creating a wild food garden is ensuring that it doesn't become a jumble, which is both unattractive and inefficient. There is no doubt that food production has a different aesthetic than other gardening styles but all the same it is not without beauty, reason or order. Just because beds need to be turned, composted and mulched doesn't mean that a productive garden should lack charm. By organising our gardens into zones, we can ensure that they are laid out to be highly productive, easy to maintain, and that they have plant associations which can be supportive in terms of pest control and nutrition.

The larger the garden, the further you can take this concept, but even in an urban or suburban situation an understanding of the broader principles of a wild food garden can be engaged to create a healthier garden.

◀ **LEFT** Creating a herb wheel in the centre of a potager, as here at Dalton's Plantation, with pollinators in the middle, is a great way to bring companion plants into your productive garden. It also makes a beautiful centrepiece.

THE FIRST RULE is to avoid simple monocultures. While monocultures are a great way to increase the yield of single crops, more complex systems — be they based on rotation or companion planting or a mix of both — tend to have a higher food yield per metreage (albeit it may be less per individual crop) than a chemically managed system. This doesn't mean that every tomato plant you grow needs to be separated into a different plot; growing in clusters is more than okay. But I want to encourage gardeners to look at the garden not in terms of each block of planting but as an interconnected system. When you choose where to plant your tomatoes you need to consider how to best support this crop's requirements — full sun and plentiful water, for example. That would dictate that you plant them close to an efficient water supply and in an open bed, where they have reduced competition for water. On the other hand, fruit trees such as pears or plums do not need frequent watering and can grow tall to reach the sunlight. They also have the potential to shade sun-hungry and thirsty annual crops such as tomatoes and so should be planted further from the house. This also makes sense when you consider how frequently they need to be harvested and fed.

> More complex patterns such as spirals may appear decorative and fussy but they actually create a broad and efficient way of increasing the range of growing conditions as well as paths in and out of the spaces.

IF YOU WISH to increase the variety of your plantings so that you have a broad range of food throughout the seasons you need to understand how to make the most effective use of growing space. Flat beds are a completely valid way to grow crops, but if you are trying to increase yield then mounding increases the growing area considerably. More complex patterns such as spirals may appear decorative and fussy but they actually create a broad and efficient way of increasing the range of growing conditions as well as creating practical paths in and out of

the spaces. Constructing climbing frames that straddle pathways can further maximise the growing plane.

Mounding does not need to be done artificially and can be built up slowly over time with intensive composting programmes and the introduction of layers of thick mulches such as straws, banana leaves and even newspaper, used in conjunction with manures and mineral sources such as seaweed.

Walls, too, should be assessed for their growing potential, and can be utilised for food production in a number of ways. Traditionally, espalier trees such as pears or apples have been trained against boundaries and climbing vines such as passionfruit or clambering crops such as zucchini or cucumber have been trained up fences or the sides of buildings. In contemporary design, modular green walls have been integrated into building design as a mechanism for urban food production. Areas of glass have even been transformed into urban office block and apartment window farms, using a hydroponic system of hanging bottles. This is hardly what would be described as 'wild gardening' but it is certainly a new approach to urbanisation that is fresher, greener and loads of fun.

Water is such an essential part of the productive garden that it makes sense to design a means of water collection that will reduce dependence on mains supply. Consideration should be given not just to water collection but also to opportunities for reuse of household wastewater. Most of the grey water from showering, washing clothes and non-greasy dishes is absolutely appropriate for our gardens, and the reuse not only will save money but also saves the wastewater charges. You do need a separate meter to measure reused water, so it can be removed from your household's bill. In some areas you may not currently be charged directly for water use but it is likely that before long you will be, and you will be grateful for the savings when this time arrives.

IN ALL GARDENS aspect needs consideration; it will dictate what you are able to grow. Even though every site has its opportunities, if you

▲ **PREVIOUS PAGES** A vegetable garden does not need to be hidden behind a screen and can be worked into the structure of a garden. Despite the seasonal nature of most vegetable gardens, they can be given permanent structure with low-clipped hedges and attractive frames. The hedges in the Woodbridge garden are buxus, but cranberries make a great edible alternative. Rosemary or blueberry are excellent for taller hedges and around the borders. Feijoa is best shared on a boundary with your favourite neighbours.

▶ **RIGHT** There's a real charm in gardener-made climbing structures. Plants almost always climb higher than you think they will so think big!

are really serious about food production you will need to be very mindful of the orientation of your site and be prepared to make major interventions, if required. Prevailing wind and exposure to sea salt could, for example, be viewed as potential obstacles but with careful planning and shelter-planting they can be mitigated and microclimates within a site created. Poor soil, too, can be redressed over time with generous applications of compost and good organic matter. However, the brutal fact is that the sun will always rise and set in the same direction and can't be manipulated by adjusting planting schemes. It should, though, be considered in our planting plans especially when deciding where to place specimen trees that may grow to overshadow this precious, renewable power pack.

Composting is the cornerstone of a productive garden. It's a sustainable means of waste management and ensures that your garden is supplying you with food that carries appropriate nutrition. While early organic ideals embraced the idea of ecologies as perfectly balanced, closed systems with an ideal equilibrium, modern thinking leans more towards the idea of nature in a state of constant change that is completely interlinked. The same applies to our gardens. It is not possible to shut out the influences that lie beyond our property boundaries: weeds, neighbours' preferences and weather patterns, for example. Instead, our gardens need to work within these settings rather than fighting against them. A productive garden will disperse seeds as well as the fruits of its labour beyond its boundary — some will go to friends and neighbours and it's a fair bet that some, at least, will be stolen by birds.

Although efforts should certainly be made to manage whatever waste we can on-site and to return it to the garden, it is likely that some external supplies will need to be brought in to keep the soil highly productive. Be it the addition of composts and mulch or trace elements, it is a simple sum: energy in must equal the energy out, and it is worth remembering that we ourselves are taking considerable energy and nutrients from our gardens which need somehow to be replenished.

Designer's guide

ZONES

THINK ABOUT DIVIDING your garden into three simple areas to get you started. The first is for high productivity. This is where you will grow annual crops that require weekly care and daily harvesting. It should be close to your main living space, and therefore convenient to access as well as being easy to water and fertilise. Raised beds (see The Natural Gardener, page 307) or even containers may be appropriate. For many gardeners this will be the main area of production. In this zone, composting would be best dealt with using a modular system such as a worm farm: clean and not smelly.

The second zone is more suited to either in-ground beds or mound gardens. This is where you will grow crops that need both space and time. Potatoes and berries are good examples as are pumpkins. Climbing frames are also of great value here for grapes or kiwifruit, vigorous growers that perform best with some space to reach their potential. While large trees may be likely to cause issues with sun, in this zone dwarf trees and climbing structures are totally appropriate and can be used to create sheltered areas for more tender plants.

In a suburban situation this is also where you might want to integrate hens, although in a smaller garden they could be just as suited to a third orchard or forest zone. Keep in mind that hens do need daily care: food, water and, of course the best bit, egg-gathering. While their waste product is invaluable as a source of nitrogen in a composting system, it does need to be gathered regularly or else flies are likely to cause problems.

In this zone it is possible to have a larger composting system capable of processing a good range of waste from chicken manure, waste plant materials, lawn clippings and 'browns' such as leaf drop or paper waste. If food scraps are kept in a closed system such as a worm

▲ **PREVIOUS PAGES** Raised beds don't have to be high to be effective. As the productive garden at Dalton's shows, a single layer of railway sleepers can be used to create all sorts of shapes and even gentle curves. Having a series of beds makes it easy to rotate your crops and reduces disease and nutrient deficiencies.

▶ **RIGHT** These Verda kitset beds at Dalton's have been 'accessorised' with simple curved frames welded from reinforced steel. These frames support the berries as they grow and make it easy to throw netting over to keep the birds off.

farm in zone one you are unlikely to have problems with rodents and other pests (in my garden the main challenge is urban possums!).

Zone three can be given a range of names, depending on the size and scale of your endeavour. This is where your tall fruit trees can be grown, with a range of woodland herbs such as comfrey, thyme and even daffodils. The main difference in approach from a contemporary orchard is the replacement of a mown lawn with a naturalised planting of companion plants that have their own uses as green mulch or nutrient miners (these are plants like comfrey and lupins that have deep tap roots that penetrate deep into the soil, bringing up otherwise inaccessible minerals). If space allows, you can even consider planting larger nut trees, just as long as you are sure that when they are fully grown — or even halfway there — they won't be stealing sun from your other two zones.

PATHS

A WELL-ORGANISED SERIES of paths is really important for a healthy edible garden. Dinner needs to be made whatever the weather, and you need to be free to move safely and effectively through the garden at any time. Gravel paths that can be replenished with fresh stone every couple of years are very effective. Regularly walked, they are easily kept free of weeds and they do not gather moss or mould and become slippery in wet weather as wood can. Pavers tend to be more expensive and can be prone to gathering weeds in the gaps and need to be relaid over time.

Pebble, too, is permeable, allowing water to flow freely through rather than gathering and sitting as it can on concrete. Paths also need to be a practical width that will easily allow a wheelbarrow to be moved through at least the main areas of the garden. Ideally, you should be able to get the barrow into all areas. A good width for most garden paths is 1200 mm, but if you are limited for space then check your minimum acceptable path size by trekking through the garden with a barrow and being realistic about the minimum width you feel comfortable carrying a load of compost through.

► **RIGHT** Stepping a garden space down even just a couple of levels can help to make an easy transition between different areas of a garden, say from vegetables to herbs and pollinators. Strong path structure is a good way to keep a garden looking smart even when the plantings are informal, as here at Woodbridge garden.

GARDEN WIDTH

WHATEVER STYLE of garden you are after, be it raised beds or winding spiral mounds, you need to consider the harvest. It may be practical to let fruit trees and climbers that you harvest seasonally grow tall, using a ladder for harvest, but generally we need to keep crops within reach. Deep beds are one of the most common mistakes beginners make, but if you've gone down this path don't despair. A small path of stepping stones through a garden bed can be interplanted with herbs such as thyme or chamomile, providing not only access but also an aromatic walkway.

STORAGE AND WORK BENCH

IF YOU ARE going to take your kitchen garden seriously you will need an area for jobs such as seed raising, taking cuttings, and even for sorting harvested seeds. It is highly valuable to have either a greenhouse or an area of covered glass, not only for propagation but also to give you the opportunity to grow the odd garden treat that you might not be able to grow outdoors in your region. Storage for garden tools and materials is also important, be it in a lean-to or a garden shed, and it is important to be able to keep equipment dry and well organised. Tidiness in the garden is really important both for efficiency and to prevent disease being spread. This applies to tools, too. Good quality tools will last a lifetime, and several generations more, if they are kept well sharpened, clean and dry.

WATERING SYSTEMS

WHATEVER WATERING SYSTEM you decide upon — tank, tap, automated, manual or a combination of all — you need to be certain that you can get water to all areas of the garden with not too much

effort. It could be as simple as having a second tap plumbed to the bottom of the garden; the cost of losing plants in a hot summer is likely to be far greater than getting the plumber in.

GROWING FRAMES

NOT ONLY ARE growing frames a really effective way of using space in the centre of garden beds, they also offer an opportunity to add some creativity to the garden and to reuse or borrow from other areas of the garden. Bamboo stakes are perfectly efficient and can be used to make all sorts of shapes for training plants upwards, but they are not the only option. Flax-flower heads can be used to make pyramid frames and flax leaves also make strong and durable rope or twine. Grapevine prunings can be woven to make cones, and driftwood has numerous uses for building in the garden. Our native ponga can be another option for a living, growing pole — as long as the climber it is hosting is not too aggressive.

COMPANIONS

THE PRODUCTIVE GARDEN'S main purpose is food supply and to provide this effectively it needs plants that will support the main crops. Fruit trees need pollinators, and therefore flowering plants aid in bringing bees to the garden. Many flowering plants such as nasturtium, calendula and marigolds will assist in pest control while woodland herbs such as comfrey and lupins can help restore nitrogen levels. They also add colour and beauty to the garden.

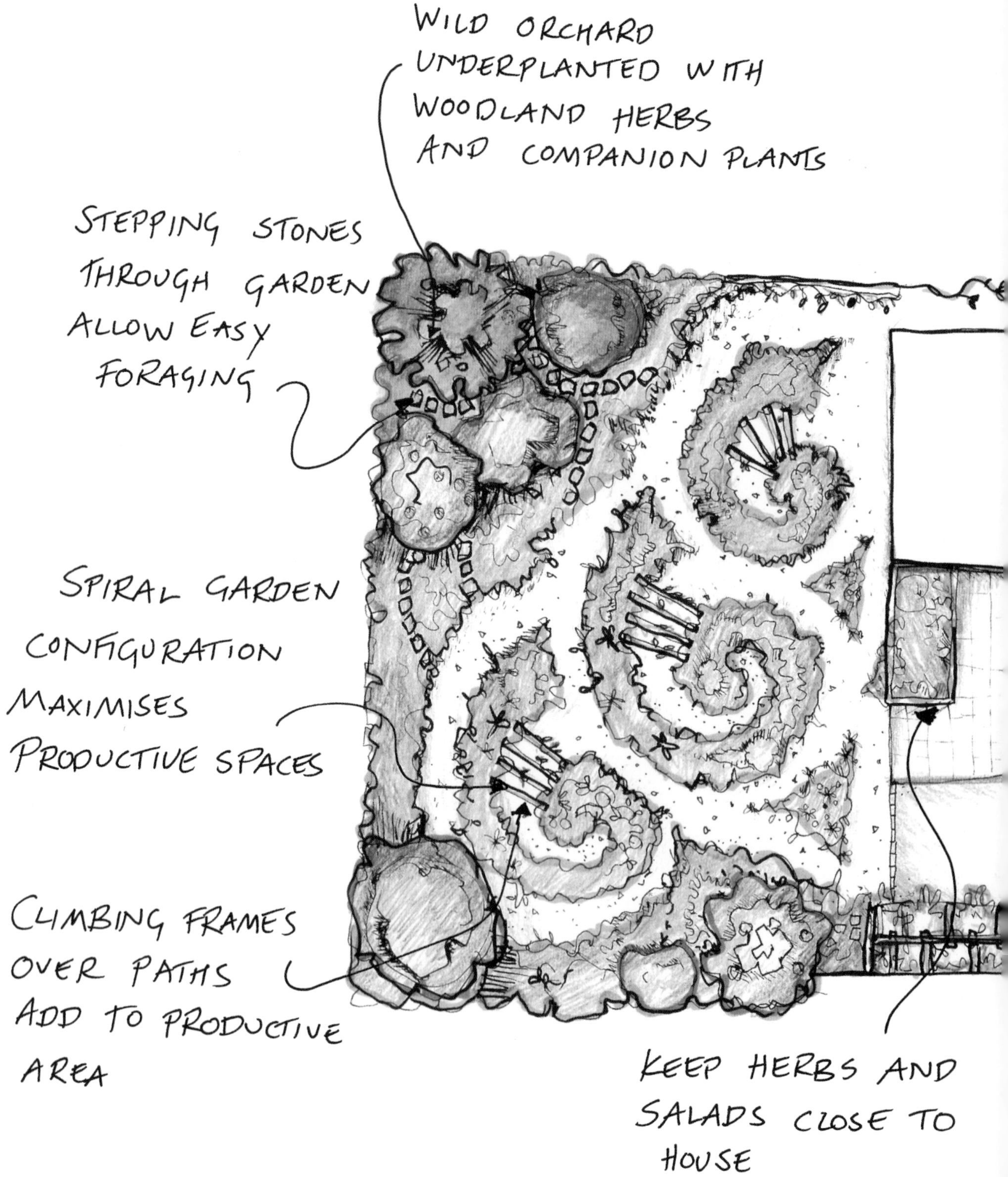

WILD ORCHARD
UNDERPLANTED WITH
WOODLAND HERBS
AND COMPANION PLANTS

STEPPING STONES
THROUGH GARDEN
ALLOW EASY
FORAGING

SPIRAL GARDEN
CONFIGURATION
MAXIMISES
PRODUCTIVE SPACES

CLIMBING FRAMES
OVER PATHS
ADD TO PRODUCTIVE
AREA

KEEP HERBS AND
SALADS CLOSE TO
HOUSE

USE ALL FENCES TO GROW FOOD WITH CLIMBERS AND ESPALIER

REUSE OLD CROCKERY OR TILES TO DETAIL PATHS, ADDING COLOUR AND CHARACTER

WILD PLANTINGS OF POLLINATORS. CREATE FLOWER GARDENS STREET SIDE

SERVICE AREA WITH GLASSHOUSE, POTTING BENCH AND COMPOSTING

Helianthus annuus
SUNFLOWER
Probably the most fun of all garden flowers. Not only popular with bees and other important pollinators, also great for getting young gardeners started.

Salvia elegans
PINEAPPLE SAGE
These nectar-rich plants are also edible and can be used in teas; reputed to help lower blood pressure and calm anxieties.

Cleome spinosa
SPIDER FLOWER
Not only a top plant for attracting beneficial insects to the garden, but also a stunning garden feature with flower heads standing one and a half metres tall.

Calendula spp.
POT MARIGOLD
Believed to assist in deterring disease in plants. Also reputed to have antiviral abilities and assist in easing cramps. Should not be taken during pregnancy.

Monarda didyma
BERGAMOT
These flowers are not only show stoppers, they also attract pollinators and have strong antiseptic properties.

Amaranthus spp.
AMARANTH
Various species have been used by many cultures for grain, as a root vegetable and for leaf.

Thymus vulgaris
THYME
An absolute favourite with honey bees. Very hardy in hot, dry conditions but will also grow on a shady site.

Lavandula spp.
LAVENDER
Another great plant for bees. There are many varieties. All need clipping back after flowering.

Tagetes spp.
MARIGOLD
Often confused with calendula. Its strong scent is said to discourage certain pests. Dig directly into the soil once flowering is over to discourage nematodes.

Echinacea purpurea
ECHINACEA
This is one of my all-time favourite plants. Should be planted in dry, free-draining soil without compost. Excellent pollinator.

Cynara cardunculus var. *scolymus*
GLOBE ARTICHOKE
Rated for its stunning silver thistle-like leaves, breathtaking flowers and, if picked before flowering, its delicious buds. Will perform in dry clay soils.

Lupinus angustifolius
BLUE LUPIN
An important green mulch. Its long tap roots bring nutrients from deeper soil into the growing region. Dig direct through soil after collecting seed.

Anthemis nobilis
CHAMOMILE
This aromatic plant can be used as a calming tea. *Matricaria recutita* and German chamomile also have medicinal properties.

Althaea rosea
HOLLYHOCK
Best grown from seed sown late autumn to give you flowers early spring. However, a spring sowing will give you another round of flowers at the end of summer.

Ocimum basilicum
BASIL
A great companion plant for tomatoes, both in the garden to discourage pests and when picked fresh as a flavour balance.

Tropaeolum spp.
NASTURTIUM
A great boundary plant in a garden to discourage pests. Both the leaves and spicy flowers are great in salads.

Symphytum officinale
COMFREY
Can be invasive if planted in your main garden, but the perfect plant for an orchard where it can be mowed occasionally, with the leaf collected for garden mulch.

Allium spp.
ALLIUM
The strong odour of plants in this family, which includes both onions and garlic, is a great deterrent for garden pests.

NORTH

Citrus spp.
CITRUS

Citrus, especially the lemon tree, used to be one of the defining plants of a kiwi backyard in frost-free areas.

Feijoa sellowiana
FEIJOA

Another kiwi classic. Feijoa season starts in late summer. Plant a hedge and get recipes for chutney and cake.

Citrus reticulata
MANDARIN

Mandarins are a long lasting fruit as birds do not like the sour skin. A tablespoon of Epsom salts once a month through the growing season does wonders.

Cyphomandra betacea
TAMARILLO

In warmer gardens this is an easy-to-grow if short-lived treat. Expect seven years of great crops before it may need replanting.

SOUTH

Diospyros virginiana
PERSIMMON

One of the great joys of this tree is its bright orange fruit, which lasts late into autumn once the leaves have fallen. Excellent feature tree.

Malus spp.
APPLE

Though apples get better the further south you go, they can be grown in most gardens. It's advisable to place hormone traps for codling moth.

Prunus persica var. *nectarina*
NECTARINE

Another stone fruit that fares far better in cooler climates.

Brassica oleracea
BRUSSELS SPROUT

The elusive brassica that needs a deep, crisp cold to really do its best. If you can grow this, brag about it!

Daucus carota
CARROT

While carrots may grow in lots of gardens, to get a true sweet flavour you need a good frost.

Solanum tuberosum
POTATO
The fun thing about potatoes is you can bury the plants as they grow to increase the root crop below. See how many you can get per plant. Harvest after flowering.

Solanum lycopersicum
TOMATO
Unbeatably the garden favourite, these summer fruits are a great starting point for any gardener.

Lactuca sativa
LETTUCE
Fresh greens are an important part of the diet and even the smallest spaces have room to grow them.

Prunus spp.
PLUM
Can be grown from north to south with great success and well worth a place in any garden. Spring flowers are an additional joy.

Phaseolus spp., *Vigna* spp., *Vicia* spp.
BEANS
Be it broad, runner or French, beans should be the first seed you try to sow as they will fill you with confidence from there on in.

Cucurbita pepo
ZUCCHINI
A highly productive crop suitable for most gardens. The secret to enjoying these is to pick them while young and sweet.

OTHER PLANTS TO CONSIDER

COMPANION PLANTS

Borago officinalis
BORAGE

Asclepias physocarpa
SWAN PLANT

Brassica juncea
MUSTARD

Coriandrum sativum
CORIANDER

Buddleia spp.
BUTTERFLY BUSH

NORTH

Ipomoea batatas
KUMARA

Capsicum annuum
CAPSICUM

SOUTH

Pastinaca sativa
PARSNIP

Prunus armeniaca
APRICOT

EVERYWHERE

Cucurbita spp.
PUMPKIN

Zea mays
CORN

Pyrus spp.
PEAR

THE NATURAL
Rooftop
Garden

We are now a mostly urban-dwelling nation and the demand for space is intense. As the bigger cities move to concentrate their metropolitan boundaries to contain sprawl and as city people decide they want to move closer to the city centre rather than being commuters in the far-flung suburbs, there's a push for higher-density living, be it in apartments, townhouses or just on smaller subdivided sections. It's not a bad move: after all, it's an effective way of concentrating resources. But the struggle is to find a way to maintain a relationship with nature, both as a source of healthy food and for the sense of well-being that comes with such connections.

The largest pot artist William Beattie ever made, by mounding hypertufa over a giant pile of mulch and then lifting the finished pot with a digger. The hypertufa and shallow nature of the bowl make this a lightweight solution to get a large tree into an otherwise barren landscape, here in Auckland's Viaduct Harbour district.

THE MAIN CHALLENGE for the urban gardener is lack of space, yet if there was ever evidence that we are at our most creative when resources are restricted then the city garden movement would be it. Overseas rooftops have been transformed into farms complete with beehives; balcony-less apartments have been fitted with window farms, hydroponic systems of growing herbs and lettuce in chains of bottles against windows. Entire buildings have been constructed and retrofitted with Patrick Blanc's living-wall systems that transform buildings into bio-diverse works of art. And abandoned city lots have been infiltrated by bands of guerilla gardeners planting seeds in the cracks of perishing concrete.

Patrick Blanc's green-wall systems are certainly one of the most significant developments in urban gardening over the last century. Blanc's background is in botany, and it's taken him three decades to fully develop his system, starting with his first attempts to grow plants from an aquarium and up onto the wall of his bedroom. His inspiration came from years of observing the natural systems that develop on the vertical planes of waterfalls, the understorey of the forest floor and in cave-like environments where slow and continuous flows of water over stone host a complex range of life.

Key to this is the layer of moss and fungus which first forms in such conditions. This spongy layer is what the Blanc system of green walls imitates with its felt base, into which plants are planted in small pockets. The system is being continually refined but essentially it's constructed around a metal frame similar to scaffolding to which the felt layer is attached. It can be retrofitted to any building. Water, including a liquid feed of nutrients, is dripped through the layer of felt and pumped back through the system.

The plants Blanc selects to grow on his walls are also important. He uses highly complex planting plans which are rich in biodiversity; if a wall is planted in a monoculture or with a limited range of species it is more vulnerable to pests and diseases. Plant material is selected for its appropriateness to the aspect of the building, which may vary from the bottom to the top of a single wall, and to the surrounding environment. This complexity is key to increasing the overall value of the green space, making it a treasure-trove for valuable species that can withstand environmental changes.

The disadvantage of Blanc's systems is that they are expensive to install and there is a high running cost, including the high water uptake. Where possible, Blanc and his teams are looking at reusing waste water from within the buildings themselves as well as collecting stormwater run-off from surrounding areas. As this becomes a reality the value of these systems will greatly increase, with walls becoming part of a site's waste management plan as well as centres for urban diversity.

The other important contribution that green spaces, be they walls or parks, make to cities is as a cooling mechanism. Before the planting of street trees was commonplace, heat levels in some overseas cities were responsible for some deaths of young children and the elderly. The introduction of street trees occurred in response, and avenues of trees are now taken for granted as an integral part of our urbanscapes. As the building heights of our cities continue to climb so does the need for greenscapes. In large cities such as London, councils are pushing for new buildings to include roof gardens as a matter of course.

ALTHOUGH LARGE-SCALE VERTICAL walls may be out of the reach of the average urban gardener, Blanc's principles have inspired a revolution in the way we view our city spaces and the direction from which we approach gardening. Versions of the vertical concept have been adapted to a wide range of situations, and with increasing resourcefulness and ingenuity. Wooden pallets, for example, have been turned on their sides, filled with soil and planted into. Hollow concrete blocks have also been turned sideways and planted into, turning narrow spaces into productive corridors. Window sills have been engaged for a number of vertical systems, making the most of the available light.

Roof gardens are steadily increasing in popularity as their many benefits become evident. The main challenge for roof gardens is the weight of the soil medium, especially when it is loaded with water. For this reason roof gardens tend to be more suited to shallow-rooting

plants that are able to grow in a lightweight and porous growing medium such as pumice or even crushed brick. Large trees are not totally out of the question but their weight needs to be accounted for in the engineering of a building and they are less likely to be appropriate when a roof garden is being installed on an existing building.

Consideration also needs to be given to the environment of a rooftop. Roofs are best compared to an alpine environment which can reach both low and high temperatures, is likely to have gravelly soils, be buffeted by high winds, and experience extreme periods of drought while also needing to be able to process water through a shallow growing medium. It is these challenges that give roof gardens a unique character. Plant selection is key, and low-growing species are the most ideal. Surprisingly, turf grass is less suitable than other groundcovers; although turf can be kept low by regular mowing, its root system ideally requires 150–200 mm of soil medium and intense watering.

Designer's guide

THINKING VERTICAL

THE MAIN CHALLENGE when you are undertaking vertical gardening of a DIY nature is the need to have a clear understanding of how you are going to water. First, it is critically important that any watering programme will not cause any harm to the structural integrity of the building or pose a health risk because it harbours moulds and fungus. You need to ensure that the surfaces are protected and that any excess water can be collected, and ideally reticulated, through the watering system. The most common fault I've noticed on some of the models that can be bought online is poor drainage. Plants need moving water, and if they are in a sealed container the water will become stagnant, leaving the plants prone to disease.

◀ **LEFT** Vertical gardens essentially mimic nature, where tiny plants, especially mosses and small ferns, establish in difficult places such as this waterfall in the Waitakere Ranges, and where opportunistic plants will take up residence, such as on this balcony in downtown Auckland. Wherever there are cracks and crevices that contain water and allow humus to build up, life will take hold in some form.

LIGHTING

TO GROW PLANTS inside or out you need an adequate source of light, ideally natural light. Standard artificial light is not beneficial as it is mainly composed of red or warm light, which is sufficient to assist flowering and fruiting in plants but will not promote lush green growth. For that, plants require adequate blue light such as is found in fluorescents. The problem is that this is the light we humans least like to live under! Specialised grow lights have been developed for greenhouse growers; they're also widely used in the drug industry. Don't let the fact that they have some illegal users put you off!

WEIGHT

VERTICAL STRUCTURES can get really heavy and it is important that the higher you go, the more carefully you calculate the weight of your structure. You need to take into account not just the dry weight of your growing medium but also the fully saturated weight. First you need to work out the volume, which is calculated by multiplying the height by the length of the structure and then multiplying this figure by the depth. This (if done in metres) will give you the cubic metre rate of your structure. A heavy soil weighs around 1600 kilograms per cubic metre wet. It is advisable to check with your product supplier what weight any particular growing medium may be as it's useful to have an initial figure to work from when you are designing a scheme. You then need to ensure that whatever walling or flooring you are attaching your structure to can take the load expected. In areas prone to earthquakes you also need to be certain that the structure is well attached to a solid wall.

PLANT SELECTION

YOU MAY BE SURPRISED by how wide the palette of plant material suited to green walls can be. Ferns are a popular choice but you should also consider large-leafed plants such as begonias, hostas and even dwarf taro. Planted on a flat plane, these would far outgrow their site but if they are grown hydroponically the reduced root size will limit the final size of the plant, making otherwise invasive plants self-limiting in this system. Something wonderful also happens when these dish-leafed plants grow on this plane as we get to appreciate the form of the leaf from an entirely fresh perspective. Edible plants are also valuable in this environment, especially perennial herbs that do not require constant renewal. You also need to consider how these will be harvested and ensure that you keep your vertical garden within the limits of your own reach.

ROOF GARDENS

ONE OF THE GREAT benefits of a roof garden is that you can use it to collect roof water that would otherwise be going into the stormwater system, using it to maintain the garden itself. A roof garden will also assist in both cooling and insulating the building itself. If you are going to go to the trouble of creating such a structure then you might as well design it so it can be accessed and utilised as an additional living space. The main challenge here is ensuring that safety barriers are appropriate, especially if your roof is at an extreme height. The views, however, will be worth the added expense. Consideration also needs to be given to the exposed conditions in this sort of environment, be it wind, sun or rain. The higher you are, the more you are going to feel it. Keep in mind, too, that umbrellas and garden furniture should ideally be tied down to avoid flying garden accessories. Access also needs to be considered, and such an area should have child safety locks. You really need to treat it with the same level of precaution that you would a pool area.

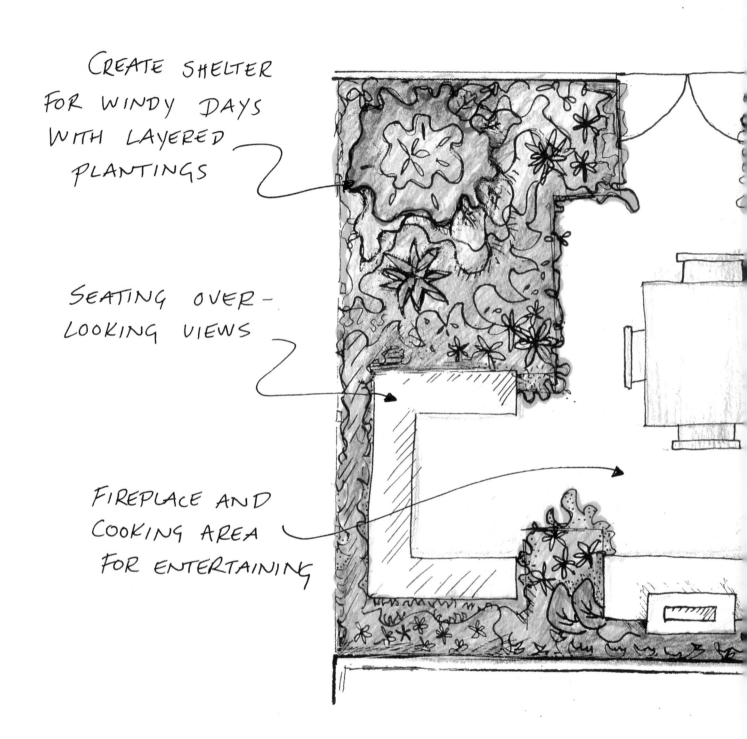

CREATE SHELTER
FOR WINDY DAYS
WITH LAYERED
PLANTINGS

SEATING OVER-
LOOKING VIEWS

FIREPLACE AND
COOKING AREA
FOR ENTERTAINING

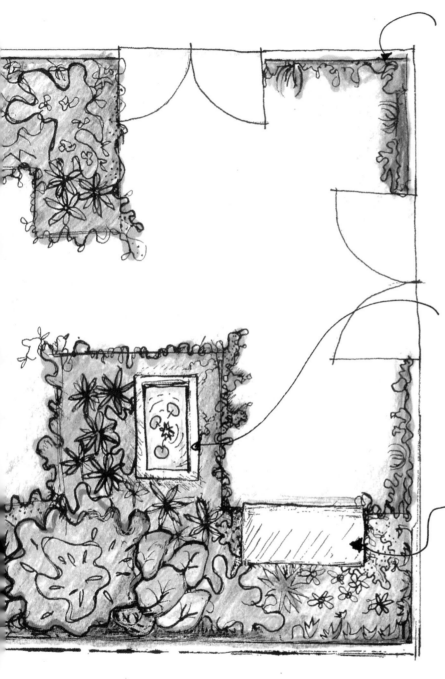

GREEN WALLS
SOFTEN BUILDINGS
AND INCREASE
PLANTING AREAS

FOCAL POINT
WITH WATER
VIEWED FROM
DIFFERENT AREAS

CREATE INTIMATE
SPACES ENCLOSED
IN PLANTING

◄ **LEFT** Even the smallest of spaces can include a complex range of species and need not look fussy. Rich greens tie this wall, which I created for the 2012 Ellerslie Flower Show, together, and the different leaf forms provide interest. Where the sun hits, plant sun lovers like this orange berry; shady edges and corners are ideal for damp-loving ferns.

GREEN WALLS

PLANT GUIDE

Adiantum hispidulum
ROSY MAIDENHAIR

This delicate-leafed fern has many appealing attributes including its pink-flushed foliage. Hardy outside but doesn't like draughts.

Pellaea rotundifolia
BUTTON FERN

Provides a beautiful dark, glossy texture to green walls that contrasts well with other plants and gives a wall depth.

Atrichum androgynum
MOSS

An important aspect of vertical landscapes. Helps to hold moisture and humus on the surface which then allow other plants to grow.

Doodia australis
PUKUPUKU, RASP FERN

A hardy fern with fine, hard leaves that flush red on new growth. Very reliable.

Nertera balfouriana
NERTERA

Wonderful filler and simple texture to plant behind more defined foliage. Will grow beautifully around the fringes of their leaves.

Elatostema rugosum
PARATANIWHA

Perfect for a shaded green wall with good irrigation, this native has wonderful fresh green and bronze leaves. Defined form also makes it ideal for a vertical wall.

Blechnum novae-zelandiae
KIOKIO
Grows naturally on clay banks with leaves that blush red as new growth develops.

Portulaca spp.
ICEPLANT
For colour, this is great in shallow gravel gardens. Will withstand dry periods.

Blechnum penna-marina
ALPINE HARD FERN
Very versatile. Performs well in sun and shade and forms dense matting that is hardy and attractive, especially when new pink growth comes through.

Blechnum minus
SWAMP KIOKIO
Similar to *B. novae-zealandiae* but smaller with purple-red leaves. Enjoys slightly moister and shadier conditions.

Gunnera prorepens
CREEPING GUNNERA
This water-loving groundcover has attractive flowers and berries. Must have a water source.

Echinops spp.
GLOBE THISTLE
This low-growing perennial loves exposed conditions and free-draining gravel soils are ideal.

Geranium 'Purple Passion'
NEW ZEALAND GERANIUM
The well-formed purple-bronze foliage of this perennial makes a nice contrast to other forms on a vertical wall.

Hylotelephium telephium
AUTUMN SEDUM
Tolerant of water restrictions, this perennial brings life and insects as well as colour to a roof garden.

Selliera radicans
REMUREMU
This coastal plant is used to tough conditions. An excellent alternative to traditional lawn and performs well in shallow soils.

Coprosma propinqua
COPROSMA
Slow to establish but once settled this groundcover loves growing over hard surfaces such as gravel mulched gardens.

Leptinella dioica
SHORE COTULA
This groundcover will happily grow on a rooftop but prefers situations where the water supply is reasonably consistent.

Aloe ferox
CAPE ALOE
Best grown in pots, especially if you wish to see it reach maturity. Given the space for root development, will happily handle the conditions.

Geranium traversii var. *elegans*
CHATHAM ISLAND GERANIUM
One of our native geraniums, this shallow-rooting perennial has the compact growth appropriate for a shallow soil medium.

Scleranthus uniflorus
CUSHION PLANT
Naturally occurring in an alpine environment, this native is ideally adapted to a rooftop environment and has suitably shallow roots.

Xeronema callistemon
POOR KNIGHTS LILY
Performs best in containers with a strong growing medium. Red plumes are formed in summer.

OTHER PLANTS TO CONSIDER

GREEN WALLS

Begonia spp.
BEGONIA

Hosta spp.
HOSTA

Ophiopogon japonicus
MONDO GRASS

Heuchera spp.
HEUCHERA

Rubus pentalobus
ORANGE BERRY

Fragaria x *ananassa*
STRAWBERRIES

Origanum vulgare
MARJORAM

Carex spp.
CAREX

Colocasia spp.
TARO

ROOF GARDENS

Sedum spp.
SEDUM

Libertia peregrinans
NEW ZEALAND IRIS

Coprosma acerosa
SAND COPROSMA

Muehlenbeckia spp.
MUEHLENBECKIA

Disphyma australe
NEW ZEALAND ICE PLANT

Pimelea prostrata
NEW ZEALAND DAPHNE

Festuca coxii
NATIVE TUSSOCK

THE NATURAL
Restored Garden

One of the first landscape designers to sculpt the landscape into seemingly natural forms was Capability Brown (Lancelot Brown) who was influenced by William Kent, the originator of the 'natural' English landscape. Both designers and their contemporaries rejected the French-styled formal gardens which had been in vogue and aspired to create a natural continuum between the garden estate and the pastoral land and woodlands beyond.

▲ **PREVIOUS PAGE** In nature plants never grow in isolation. This native clematis has spent decades clambering up the forest greats into the sun.

▶ **RIGHT** When including stone in a garden it is always the cracks that are hardest to deal with. You can fill them with pebbles and smaller fragments but also think of planting. These are the special spots in nature where plants like to linger. If you don't choose what will grow there, opportunists will take root.

CAPABILITY BROWN WAS famous for throwing handfuls of seeds over his shoulder in order to decide the layout of a grove of trees. Though seemingly random, his reasoning was clear — and an excellent example of a gardener's attempt to recreate the accidental beauty and balance of nature in the gardens of great estates, surrounded by an English countryside of gentle, rolling hills worked for pastoral agriculture.

This very English countryside aesthetic was adopted by European settlers in their attempt to tame New Zealand's wild landscape into a little England, a process that virtually erased a unique landscape at record speed. In many cases little thought was given to the natural state or pattern of the land. A swamp was to be drained, streams cleared to the banks, and even mountainous country turned to pasture. The results have varied from regrettable to disastrous.

But as our relationship with the land has deepened, and as we have come to have a greater understanding of the value of our unique natural environments, we have begun to relinquish the edges of our farms — the wetlands and the coastal strips — encouraging them back to what stood before this intense period of clearance. How we approach such restorations depends on the scale of a site, and, in some ways, on how we define nature.

It was once believed that nature had a perfect 'balance' that we had somehow interrupted. But now the more general view is that nature is constantly changing; along with the impact of exotic species and human habitation it's not possible to simply return it exactly to its presumed original state. It is, however, possible to give our native species an advantage, ensuring that these unique plants have a chance to win the competition for occupation that will carry on with or without us.

THERE ARE A RANGE of different approaches to the restoration of a landscape, each with value and interesting in its own right. My first introduction to such a project was through my father's stories of his old climbing friend Hugh Wilson, who had undertaken to be caretaker to a unique piece of land on Banks Peninsula. The management of

Hinewai, which was surrounded by farmland, was considered radical for its time. Rather than replanting the land, Hugh's approach was to allow a natural process of restoration. Gorse, an aggressive pest on the surrounding farmland, was allowed to remain as a nursery plant to shelter the burgeoning bush. This outraged local farmers, who saw the project as a threat to their livelihood (if the gorse spread to their pasture) and an absurd abandonment of land that hard work had developed into pasture. Various battles with farmers and the local council ensued before a compromise was agreed: the boundaries of this private reserve land had to be kept clear of gorse. Twenty years on, the project has proven a great success. The approach is based on the notion of 'passive' restoration, but it's passive only insofar as native plants are allowed to naturalise. The reserve is very actively managed, especially in the area of pest control: possums, rats and wild goats have all been energetically repressed if not eliminated.

Pest control is absolutely key to restoration, whatever your approach. Such is the damage that introduced species cause to particular birdlife, and also plants, that it should be a cornerstone of land management. The challenge, however, is that your programme may be intensive but if your neighbours are not combatting pests on their land then you are going to have repeat incursions by unwanted visitors. Even in our inner city backyard we are frequently visited by possums, and rats and mice are certainly as much an urban issue as they are a rural one. This is why our island sanctuaries are such a critical part of the conservation estate: they offer a natural border, making them an ideal place to reintroduce endangered species. Pest-proof fences have also been developed with huge success at a range of mainland 'sanctuaries'.

For most private landowners pest control should be considered a community task, and it is best to combine your efforts with those of the Department of Conservation and local and regional councils, and to draw on the advice of groups such as Forest and Bird that may be working in your area.

In conjunction with this you need to decide what your approach

▶ **RIGHT** Flowering kowhai bring a revegetating garden not just the song of happy birds but the abundance of seed the birds carry with them, pre-fertilised and ready for the drop. The closer your garden is to virgin bush the more unique their droppings will be.

to the area that you wish to restore will be. A process like Hugh Wilson's at Hinewai works best if an area has source bush or wetlands, areas that retain key species from which seed will naturally spread. The more rich and diverse this source patch, the more likely you will have success on a larger scale. In areas where there is little native flora you are best advised to plant, en masse, establishment species that will start a complicated process that nature will follow through on.

Flax and manuka are good examples of these stage one species. Not only will they help to outpace the growth of weeds but they also provide a source of food for native insects and birds. In most situations the birds will come to this food source, bringing with them seed from other areas. Some of this will, of course, contain exotic plants such as cherries, palms, wattle, tobacco plant and privet, but there will also be a large proportion of native species — and the hope is that these will establish with little more help required from us apart from some weeding in the early years.

Water, too, can be used to spread seed. With this in mind, restoration of waterways can be started at the head of the river or stream, with the hope that your efforts will be carried downstream in time.

UNDERSTANDING THE LAND and its natural water patterns is as important in a process of revegetation as it is in any garden setting. Everything from the contour, the proximity to the sea, the soil type and your local climate will have an influence, just as they do in any other type of gardening. All these factors will also indicate the most likely natural ecology that stood before the land was cleared.

There is still so much for us to learn about this process; mankind's historical efforts have been in taming the landscape rather than restoring wilderness, and so in many ways this is new territory for us. While many societies have seen the benefits of preserving areas of wilderness, actually *reversing* the effects of human colonisation is a new frontier.

Central to this is our understanding of nature, an acceptance that whatever our idealised view may be, there is not a perfect balance in

► **RIGHT** Gullies are of little use to us, but give them over to nature and they cleanse water, restore diversity, create corridors for birdlife and desirable insects and can create bridges for our eyes to views beyond.

which it stands still, crystallised in a utopian ideal. Instead it is a pulsing changing force, where species compete for territory and survival. While we will never be able to erase the radical shifts in the ecosystems that our occupation has unleashed, we can — one square metre at a time — shift the competitive balance back in favour of the treasure trove of species unique to our shores before too many more disappear.

Designer's guide

LAND SELECTION

IN THEORY ANY PIECE of land can be planted with natives but revegetation is not just a native planting. It is instead a slow and measured partnership between the land's guardian and a natural process. The greatest success will be had with land that already has some conservation value in terms of a stand of existing bush, either within it or close to (ideally touching) its boundaries.

Second to this is waterways and swampy land. The value in water is not just in the unique species that occupy this niche habitat but in the ability of these species to filter contaminated water from rural or urban runoff. Every small stream connects to a complex and valuable water resource, feeding large rivers, lakes and, finally, the ocean. Restoring the seams of this web alone can sustainably reduce the impact of pollution, not just from farming and urban settlements but in some cases even heavy industry.

Other areas of importance to revegetate are the 'seams' of our landscape such as locations where the sea meets the land and where plains meet steep cliffs and unstable hills. These are areas that may have lesser value to us as productive land but provide a large range of environments for a diverse number of species.

◀ **LEFT** This photo shows well how plantings age and change over time. The under-canopy of nikau and tree ferns is quite different to the mature plantings of cordyline and karo, which are reaching the end of their lives.

APPROACH

YOU NEED TO DECIDE what method you are going to use to encourage revegetation. First is the passive path, where you allow nature seemingly complete control and let species re-establish at their own pace. While this may seem an easy hands-off approach, it requires careful management, first in controlling aggressive pests that will harm newly establishing plant species, be they possums, weeds or livestock. You also need to consider surrounding land use and the impact that this change in land use may have on your own or your neighbours' livelihoods.

Once a forest begins to develop, you also may decide that there are advantages in introducing some key species that may be unlikely to establish naturally because they are rare in the area or are slow to produce seed. The more consideration given to all these factors in the planning stages, the more likely your efforts will be well rewarded.

Planting at least the first generation of transition plants is probably the most popular method. On exposed sites it seems that the best approach is to plant directly into existing pasture, not clearing the grass, even around the planting area. Not only does the grass ensure that land is kept stable as the new plantings mature, it also helps to retain water. Of course the grass is competing for water, but nothing results in greater water loss per square metre than exposed soil. If the plants are established in a season of high rainfall, the roots will establish to a good depth that allows them to compete well with the remaining pasture at times when water is scarce.

In more sheltered areas, trials suggest that wood chip used as mulch is highly effective. It reduces competition from weeds, retains good moisture levels, and its decomposition creates warmth that greatly aids growth.

In my opinion, plastic weedmat should always be avoided. Even in its more breathable forms it damages soil development, and in the end new soil forms on the surface, making it redundant anyway. If you do wish to use a form of matting you are best advised to select a biodegradable product. There are many on the market, made of

▶ **RIGHT** At the edge of existing bush there are very select plants that will grow well. Renga renga and anemanthele both enjoy the warmer but sheltered fringes between bush and a more open aspect.

everything from cardboard to sheep dags, that will break down and in time improve soil quality in the same way that a wood or bark mulch will.

SUCCESSIONAL PLANTING

PLANT SELECTION will vary depending on the conditions and aspect of your site but generally you will always need to introduce species in a series of stages. Stage one plants, be they on a large rural block or in a home garden, need to be hardy and competitive to successfully outcompete weeds and are classed as first-generation planting. Whether it's a hot sunny site, an area prone to frost or a site exposed to coastal winds, planting 'shelter' plants first can make a huge difference to what you will be able to grow, given time. It is a good reminder that we can reshape our environment significantly, with clever plantings turning seemingly hostile landscapes into wonderlands.

ECO-SOURCING

THERE ARE NOW plant nurseries in most parts of the country that grow locally specific varieties, unique to each region. The more we learn about our native plants, the more we discover the differences within species from one end of the country to the next. The purpose of eco-sourcing — planting plants grown from seed, tissue culture, or cuttings that originated in your local area — is to preserve these differences. There are several reasons for this. Firstly, if a pohutukawa tree from Northland is planted in Tauranga, its seed will cross with other pohutukawa in the region, introducing differences in flower colour, form and perhaps even climatic hardiness to the gene pool. This has the potential to alter the local gene pool with results that may range from slight to significant. It could be as subtle as a change in colour, but as we cannot be sure of the potential impact, botanists encourage us to plant local. Of course, for centuries seed has drifted from population to population via

birds, oceans and rivers — and will continue to do so. However, there is great advantage in planting species that have adapted to a specific environment. Hardiness is as good a reason as any to take this path.

INTEGRATION

WHILE MANY LANDOWNERS are happy to see areas of land put aside for conservation, most will need to maintain areas for productive use, be it a working farm, nursery, industry, orchard or lifestyle block. It is likely that exotic plantings may be an important aspect of this mixed land use. It may be that you simply wish to grow a flower garden for cut flowers or to maintain heritage plants on a site. There is no reason why this relationship can't be symbiotic, as long as you are considered about the species you plant and on the look out for any that may develop into weeds. Always check local weed lists and avoid species known to be aggressive and invasive. Avoid, also, weak species that are dependent on sprays and chemicals for survival. Fence protected areas from any livestock on your or neighbouring properties. Give as much thought to the areas surrounding the reserve and how they can be most productively and easily managed as the reserve itself, and make sure any developments such as housing are done in suitable positions. The better designed and well integrated the whole site, the greater success you will have managing the project. Consider also the impact a forest will have on the living environment. If you wish the bush to have an extended lifespan which lasts generations, the more consideration you have given to the ongoing economics and appeal of the site, the more value the property will have in the future.

ACCESS

IT IS WORTH considering the possibility of paths or boardwalks through the site. They can allow you to move freely through the area without

◀ **LEFT** *Phormium cookianum* (mountain flax) with clipped *Muehlenbeckia astonii* and *Lobelia angulata*. Mountain flax is far better suited to gardens close to living areas than the larger *P. tenax*. Muehlenbeckia and other divaricating natives like corokia respond well to clipping and shaping. *Lobelia angulata*, until recently known as *Pratia angulata*, associates well with water and given the chance will happily clamber into a water feature.

damaging planted areas when monitoring weeds, pests and your new forest. Maintaining a relationship with this nature's garden is both the reward and an important part of gaining an understanding of the process you have undertaken. Paths and tracks need to be established early on, as they are a challenge to 'retrofit'.

They'll help you to get out into the heart of your project in years to come, and they will bring great pleasure. In some ways your most important role is as a witness and observer and, ideally, recorder of the process. As more interesting plants begin to establish you can both help to protect these newcomers while they improve their numbers and discover some of their secrets along the way. You will also find friends in the birdlife that will quickly occupy your sanctuary, and as they become familiar with you, you'll find them following your tracks.

ECONOMICS AND MAINTENANCE

LIKE ANY UNDERTAKING in life, careful planning and realistic goals are tantamount to success. Before you undertake a project you should consider the ongoing time required for management and the financial costs of preserving a landscape, just as you would if you were considering grazing cows or planting trees for forestry. These can be reclaimed in carbon credits but it also might be worth considering a set-up that is self-supporting in other ways, too. It may be that you will have the greatest success if you set aside smaller areas of land, at least initially, while keeping others as an income stream that allows ongoing management. It also doesn't hurt to practise with small sections before you develop larger projects. It is also important to consider your age and fitness when embarking on these projects. Often restoring a block of land is a retirement dream, but remember that working the land in any way takes physical strength. You'll need to ensure that you have the physical temperament to carry you through even in the wet cold winter months. The reward will be a legacy that will be treasured by generations to come.

AREAS FOR REVEG
IDEALLY LINK WITH
EXISTING BUSH
TO HELP
SEED SPREAD

PATHS FOR
PLEASURE AND
MANAGEMENT

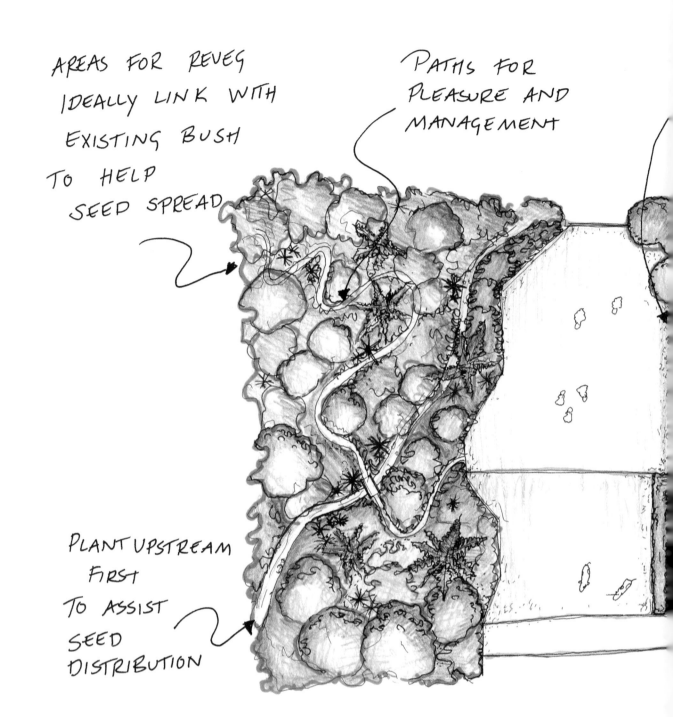

PLANT UPSTREAM
FIRST
TO ASSIST
SEED
DISTRIBUTION

HAHA FOR
SEAMLESS TRANSITION
TO LANDSCAPE

DECK OVERLOOKS
VIEWS BEYOND

EXOTIC TREES
AND GARDENS
CLOSE TO HOUSE
IF DESIRED

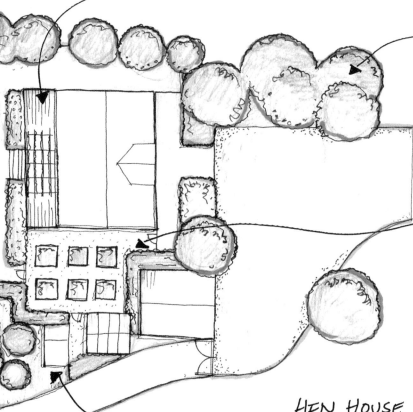

ENCLOSE KITCHEN
GARDEN AND
GREENHOUSE TO
PROTECT FROM WAND-
ERING STOCK

HEN HOUSE IN
ORCHARD SO
CHOOKS CAN
RUN FREE

MAINTAIN
WIDE ACCESS
TO BOTTOM
PADDOCKS

Metrosideros spp.
POHUTUKAWA

M. excelsa is an important tree in areas that may be vulnerable to erosion, particularly in coastal areas. Important for birds and bees.

Blechnum minus or
Blechnum novae-zelandiae
BLECHNUM

Hardy ferns that grow well on clay banks where other plants may struggle. Attractive red flush on the foliage.

Cortaderia fulvida or
Cortaderia richardii
TOETOE

Too large for most gardens, in a rural setting, particularly a coastal one, toetoe is ideal. Great for sandy soils.

Pseudopanax arboreus
WHAUWHAUPAKU

Hardy small tree that provides good cover on barren land, especially south-facing areas.

Paesia scaberula
SCENTED FERN

Considered a weed in pastoral areas but its tolerance of full sun makes it a great hardy groundcover where revegetation is required.

Corokia spp.
COROKIA

The berries of corokia are attractive to native wildlife including some of our lizards.

Leptospermum scoparium
MANUKA

A naturally occurring primary species. Plantings of manuka alone will see restoration of bush where a good seed source is nearby.

Coprosma robusta or
Coprosma propinqua
COPROSMA

Berries are attractive to wildlife and an effective weed suppressor.

Cordyline australis
CABBAGE TREE

Very attractive to birds, which assist in seed distribution. Grows in wide-ranging conditions.

Sophora microphylla
KOWHAI
Excellent tree for drawing bird species which will bring other seed to the area of revegetation. There are many varieties: choose one that is endemic to your area.

Pittosporum crassifolium
KARO
Great bird food. Excellent for coastal situations. Flowers from spring to the start of summer.

Hoheria populnea
HOUHERE
Fast-growing tree that is short-lived (ten years) but an important food supply for native wood pigeons.

Kunzea ericoides
KANUKA
Often mistaken for manuka, kanuka is generally taller and softer to touch.

Dodonaea viscosa
AKEAKE
Another good source of food for birds. Somewhat spindly, will perform better if trimmed.

Melicytus ramiflorus
MAHOE
Easily propagated from cuttings and hardy to most situations across the country. An all-rounder.

WATERWAYS

Cyperus ustulatus
GIANT UMBRELLA SEDGE
Excellent for wet zones and stream-side planting.

Coprosma virescens
MINGIMINGI
Hardy species with berries for insects, birds and other wildlife.

Phormium tenax
FLAX
Very attractive to birds and effective for erosion control. Hardy to most conditions.

Hebe spp.
HEBE
Good source of nectar for birds and insects and suited to a wide range of environments. *H. Stricta* is especially good in waterways.

Astelia spp.
WHARAWHARA
Select variety depending on conditions, whether coastal, swamp or banks.

OTHER PLANTS TO CONSIDER

BUSH/FOREST

Carex lessoniana
CUTTY GRASS, RAUTAHI

Aristotelia serrata
WINEBERRY

Acaena microphylla
SCARLET PIRIPIRI

WATERWAYS

Carex virgata
SWAMP SEDGE

Carex lessoniana
CUTTY GRASS, RAUTAHI

Astelia grandis
SWAMP ASTELIA

Schoenoplectus tabernaemontani
KAPUNGAWHA

Baumea articulata
JOINTED TWIG RUSH

Juncus gregiflorus/pallidus/ sarophorus
WIWI

Carex secta
SEDGE, PUKIO
A fresh green grass that is both attractive and easy-care.

Typha orientalis
RAUPO
A vigorous wetland plant that changes dramatically through the seasons, from attractive velvet-brown flower heads to fluffy white cotton-like seeds.

Apodasmia similis
OIOI
Important plant for water filtration. Will tolerate dry periods as well as marginal water zones.

Ficinia nodosa
KNOBBY CLUB RUSH
Particularly suited to coastal wetlands. Will handle wet and dry extremes.

► **RIGHT** A careful planting of smaller natives close to a house will bring the bush into the domestic environment without feeling too enclosing.

THE NATURAL
Coastal
Garden

Whether they are in the north or south, the west or the east, coastal gardeners everywhere share the same challenges. Here on the edge of the land the weather is changeable and often the earth is unstable. Be it dunes moving in and out or cliffs crumbling, the coast is as tough as it is undoubtedly beautiful.

▲ **PREVIOUS PAGES** Flax are excellent for sandy banks or coastal wetlands where little else may grow. Consider a circle of tall *Phormium tenax* to create an efficient windbreak.

This gravel garden shows many species suited to the poor soils of the coastal environment that deliver colour. *Corokia* 'Dark Spire' blends beautifully with catmint and salvias, highlighted by the silvery spongy form of *Calocephalus brownii.*

▶ **RIGHT** The late Derek Jarman's famous garden on the coast of Kent, near Dungeness, shows the intensity of colour and texture that can be achieved in an environment that is both arid and hit by salty winds. His garden includes Californian poppies, santolina, phlomis and verbascum.

THE SALT, TOO, takes its toll on many plants. Salt is an effective herbicide in high doses, and sandy soils retain little water or nutrients. So, even if a plant's roots are lucky or strong enough to take hold and cling to the fine soil, there is little for them to survive on. And it's not just plants that the garden designer needs to consider: paints and surfaces wear quickly in salt winds, and metals are rapidly corroded.

While these are the challenges of the seaside gardener, to their advantage is what the sea delivers. From seaweed and driftwood to flotsam and jetsam, what the ocean yields to the shoreline can be a garden designer's delight. And it is possible to ameliorate the challenges of a shore-edge environment. Careful consideration of a site and strategic planting can provide sheltered corners and send winds up and over hedges to the hills beyond. Hollows can be furrowed, and soil can, over time, be enriched with nutrients and given body by planting with rich organic matter layered in old newspapers. Every successive layer of a garden makes way for another as the roots of one plant grip at the soil, collecting debris for the next generation of plants.

To garden well on the coast you need to be determined, as well as responsive and open to grabbing the opportunities thrown to you. An artistic temperament seems ideally suited to these circumstances. The late Derek Jarman's Prospect Cottage in Dungeness, Kent, is a famous example. The artist and filmmaker moved to a small cottage in this remote community when he was diagnosed with HIV. The garden he created is simple and unusually beautiful. All the plantings are low, in keeping with the surrounding low-lying landscape. It's planted in the warm gravel, and what the garden lacks in height is made up for in colour.

The structure of the garden is mostly formed by flotsam and jetsam that Jarman collected over time. Circles of shingle and driftwood totems create anchors and edges around the drifty planting. Colours that could seem garish in a city garden are perfect for this harsh environment. Anchors, floats, and even an old fishing vessel form part of the garden,

referencing place. The garden was Jarman's complete rejection of the modernist ideal of simplicity and pure function. While the planting may appear wild, there is a clear arrangement in the colours and forms that surround the black house.

Closer to home, at the mouth of the Whanganui River, Rick Rudd, one of this country's leading ceramic artists, has crafted an equally incredible garden, Elements. Open to visitors by appointment, Rudd's garden is sculpted into the landscape. The garden has been terraced using different arrangements of collected materials, mainly from the beach, and concrete work. It is certainly a one-off and radical response to the surrounding landscape. The planting is entirely native and within the sweeps of hardy coastals such as coprosma and toetoe he has also gathered collections of rare and endangered plants.

The garden may appear wild and the walls may slope at unconventional angles, but there is also considered order in this garden. Simple sweeps of plants such as bulrush in the swampy areas and simple drifts of flax reflect not just the careful and deliberate planning of the garden but also how natives themselves grow along the coast, huddling together in groups. The details of the garden range from plant material to collections of polished glass, shells and stones that are carefully sorted into arrangements close to the house and contained in circular concrete frames.

BOTH THESE GARDENS engage the coast in a dramatic and original way but this is not the only approach. It is possible to maintain a sense of connection with the coast while creating sheltered microclimates hidden within the garden that can be used when the winds are wild and to grow unexpected delights. The best example of this that I have come across was on the island of Tresco in the Isles of Scilly, off the coast of Cornwall. Here, in the mid-1830s, a transformation into a wonderful example of a microclimate began in the ruins of an old abbey that had been abandoned in the sixteenth century. I was taken here when on the search for plants for the 100% Pure New Zealand garden at the Chelsea

Flower Show in 2006. James Fraser, an expat New Zealander and plantsman based in London, had been curious about why the Cornish coast was so ridden with New Zealand natives, and had been pointed by a local nurseryman in the direction of Tresco.

On arrival we were amazed to find nikau, pohutukawa, kauri and large clumps of xeronema flourishing on a hillside paradise. Just ten minutes up the other side of the garden, the stony soil was barren except for gorse and bramble.

Augustus John Smith, who leased the islands from the Crown, was the man responsible for such a transformation. In his attempts to establish gardens he saw the need to create shelter belts of gorse and other salt-hardy plants. This was a decision that was to set the stage for an amazing garden that emerged over several generations.

Added to this story was his management of the islands. He established a very forward-thinking education system and ensured that all the children in the area were well-educated. In fact parents who failed to send their children to school were heavily fined. This, and the fact that they were island-bound, created a generation of seamen who quickly rose up the naval ranks. In gratitude to Augustus, sailors returned to the island with plant material from all round the world including New Zealand, Australia and South Africa. So the shelter belts on the island are mostly native New Zealand olearia, and within its walls is an island which is other-worldly.

What these three gardens show us is that limitations sometimes require us to think further and to create something which is truly special. A coastal garden should not be seen as limited and difficult but rather as an opportunity to expand our horizons.

> Limitations sometimes require us to think further and to create something which is truly special. A coastal garden should not be seen as limited and difficult but rather as an opportunity to expand our horizons further.

Design Guide

HORIZONS

ONE OF THE MOST DESIRABLE aspects of a coastal garden is not just the sea itself but the opportunity to engage in an uninterrupted view to the horizon beyond. If your landscape design can engage with this, the effect can be quite dazzling. Be it water that reaches out to the sea and vanishes at the pool edge, or a patio or deck that appears to float, these illusions are made all the more dramatic with the ocean dazzling beyond. When you lay out hard landscaping features, the line of the horizon deserves as much consideration as the line of the house. Our eyes are immediately drawn to this as a reference point, and whether your lines lead to it or create a tension by running against, or at angles to it, the relationship should be deliberate.

EXPOSURE

I HAVE VISITED many homes along the coast where a deck leads to a stunning view and yet is so exposed to the sun and prevailing winds that you'll never see anyone on it. In a coastal environment humans need shelter as much as plants. This does not mean ignoring views. It could be as simple as stepping down into an entertaining area or creating a walled garden with windows that open to the views. Views can be just as dramatic when they are unexpectedly revealed.

Shade is also an important consideration. Umbrellas aren't always practical in an area with strong prevailing winds. Louvre technologies that can be adjusted to let more or less light through are an expensive but practical response to an area close to a house, but beyond the house you can consider a response as simple as a single shade tree with a built-in table beneath.

◄ **LEFT** A simple coastal garden where low plants keep their heads down against the wind.

SOILS

CONDITIONING THE SOIL should be part of your design plan. How much work you wish to put into this will greatly determine how broad a palette of plants you can select from, but generally all plants will enjoy at least a little tender care along the way and improving the soil quality so it can hold at least some organic matter will not only help retain nutrients but also greatly improve water retention. Layering newspaper, compost and sheep pellets into holes at planting time is very effective, and several thick layers are ideal. The newspaper can be used not just at the base of the hole but also around the sides so your precious soil medium doesn't wash out the edges. You can also plant out in biodegradable pots, which will help to retain quality as the roots of the plant establish into the soil. But you should still use a layer of newspaper and some enriched soil on the outside to encourage the roots to push through the pot into the soil beyond as it breaks down.

Mulching with seaweed works well, too, and a daily walk to the beach bringing a bucket-load home will have most soils improved within a year. In the dry season it should be rinsed of salt, but through periods of high rainfall you needn't bother as it will get quickly cleaned by nature.

GATHERINGS

NOT ONLY CAN seaweed be stolen from the shore, but the sea throws up all sorts of wondrous things. We are all familiar with beach treasure: battered and polished by waves and the weight of water, broken bottles turn into jewels; wood, too, is shaped and can be salvaged to make sculpture or garden furniture. Then there's bones, industrial material, wreckage, children's toys, bottle tops … A clothes-hanger tightly threaded with shells can be twisted into a meaningful shape and hung from a tree. Washed-up rope strung between driftwood and threaded with brightly coloured plastic objects could guide an informal path to

the beach. As much as gathering it's a process of sorting, of rearranging a random assortment of objects into an ordered collection that defines the garden and creates a story linking it to a place in time.

MATERIAL

I CERTAINLY HAVE a preference for natural materials in the landscape, mainly because of the honest way they weather. This weathering process is most extreme in a coastal environment and when you select material you need to consider how it will change, whether you mind the weathered look that is inevitable, and whether there's a practical and affordable means of staving it off.

A hard stone will wear well but a soft stone may be worn by salty winds over time. Bare timber will silver or can be kept fresh if it is regularly stained or oiled. Painted timber used to be soft-wearing but modern advances mean that paints will endure most circumstances for a time.

Colour should be strong: either deep dark tones or cheerful and bright ones, or even a combination of the two. The muted tones of suburbia are best avoided. This is not a place where timidity rules.

Concrete is reasonably inert and durable, although if you are colouring concrete it is worth sealing it after an acid wash to reduce staining. Mixed through with shells and pebbles and exposed, concrete has the advantage of providing a rough, slip-free tread.

Metal will corrode unless you are using a stainless steel. If you are thinking of metal balustrades, make sure the metal is marine grade and take extra care to check that all the screws and joins are too. If you like the corroded, distressed look, try Cor-Ten steel, which was developed for the marine industry and is designed to rust on the surface. But be warned, the rust will run and stain other surfaces.

Sometimes all that's needed is the occasional boardwalk through loose shingle and pebble beds.

CREATING SHELTER

BE IT A WALL OR PLANTING, one of the challenges of creating a shelter belt is ensuring that the shelter belt itself doesn't get whipped apart by prevailing winds. If you are going to build, think weighty. Stone walls are ideal; built well, they will stand up to the environment for decades. Timber walls such as trellis can be problematic: because they are so light a strong wind will lift them unless they are very securely built. Posts are inclined to sink in sandy soils, and if there is a prevailing wind it doesn't take long for them to develop a windswept lean.

It is also important to ascertain the direction of the winds you wish to protect your garden from. These can change with the seasons, and it can be advisable to take a good period of time to get to know your site before you do anything substantial. If you are new to an area, talking to neighbours and observing what they've done to create shelter is really valuable. But remember that every site can have its own peculiarities. Looking at plant material, especially established trees, can be a reliable source of information. The harsher the environment, the more telling it will be, but look for a general lean on trunks and the shape of the canopy.

Plant selection is critical. Natives such as olearia make wonderful hedges and are used to growing in coastal conditions. Take into account, though, that your hedge may also end up leaning away from the prevailing winds. You may wish to set it forward an extra metre from a living space to allow for a bit of movement over time. You can also set up some temporary shelter to support the hedge as it grows; shade cloth strung across posts is ideal for this. The cloth should be set upon the side away from the wind and should not be higher than the plants. Consider it a support rather than a screen, and once the hedge begins to join and form its own support you can take it down and reuse it in other areas.

► **RIGHT** With its pohutukawa, large specimen of Poor Knights lily and cabbage trees this could well be a shot from a New Zealand garden, but instead it is on the island of Tresco, where they call cabbage trees Cornish palms. This dry hillside garden is surrounded by shelter belts but it's also in the sunniest area of the island; site selection is key if you want to buck the odds.

PATHS

IF YOU ARE living on the coast it is likely that you will have a path either leading to the beach itself or to a quick route there. Unlike paths in a suburban garden that are likely to be hard surfaced and generally level, it is most likely that a path leading to the beach is going to amble and will be defined by the terrain.

Boardwalks are a popular choice as they simply float above the ground and are a good way of dealing with awkward levels. A concrete path is likely to buckle and sink on sandy soils and can also become covered in sand as the topography changes.

In many circumstances all that is needed is a track, and there is nothing more fun to build. The first stage is about discovering the most practical route, be it through dunes or down a bank. I would recommend you walk it a few times, putting in markers (such as brightly coloured rags in a tree) and finding out if there are any tempting shortcuts. In many cases simply walking a track is the best way to form it. You can work out as you go any steep parts that may need some simple railway-sleeper steps and try placing the sleepers out before you secure them in place.

Look, too, for beautiful views and consider making small clearings, placing a seat or even building a viewing platform. If the path is muddy or wet, you can improve the drainage by adding a layer of gravel, pumice or shell. Avoid river pebbles unless they are flat as they are inclined to roll underfoot and don't compact as well over time. Think, too, about the surface of the path if it is likely to be used by small children running barefooted. If this is the case it may be that nothing is more appropriate than a bed of soft sand.

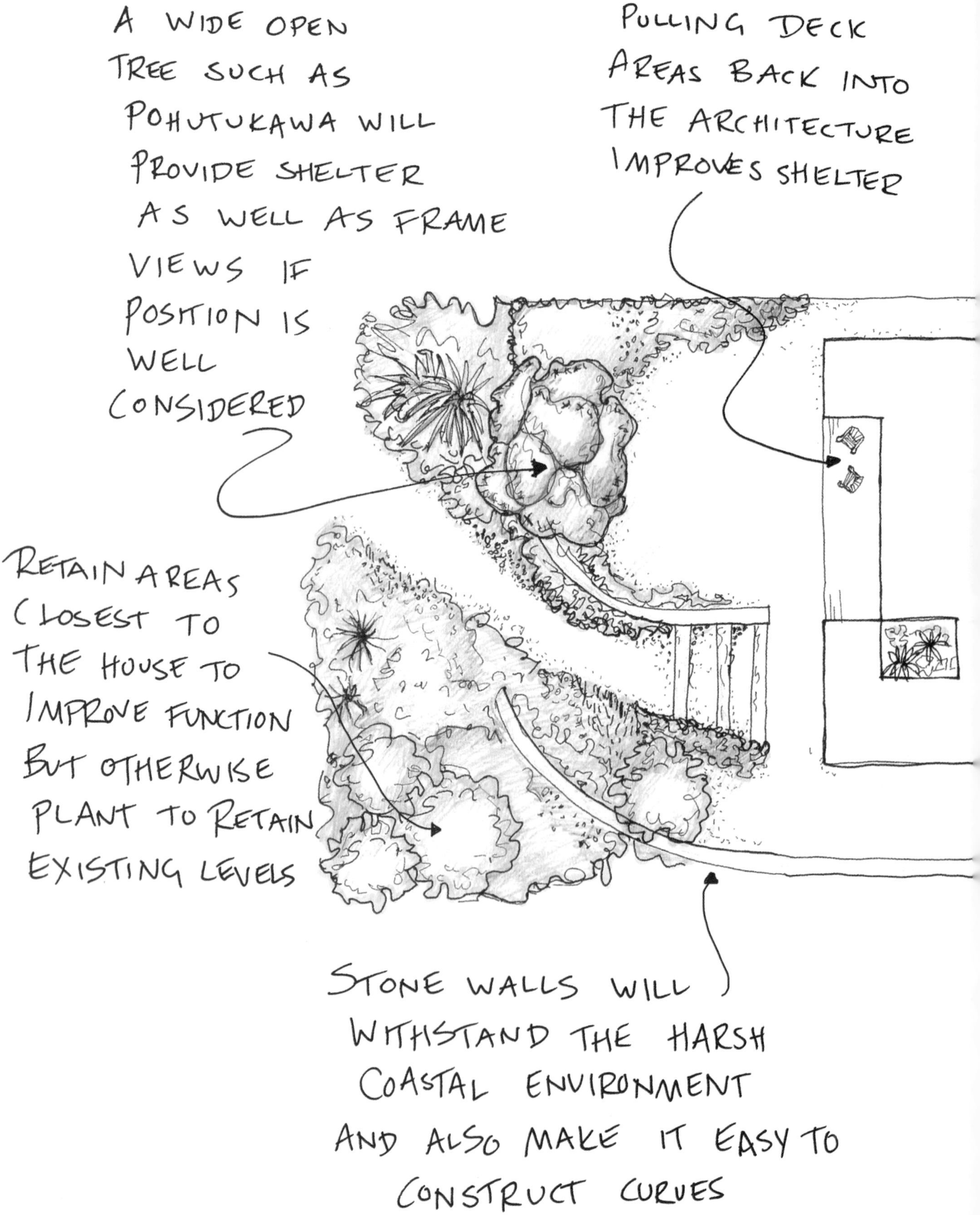

A WIDE OPEN
TREE SUCH AS
POHUTUKAWA WILL
PROVIDE SHELTER
AS WELL AS FRAME
VIEWS IF
POSITION IS
WELL
CONSIDERED

PULLING DECK
AREAS BACK INTO
THE ARCHITECTURE
IMPROVES SHELTER

RETAIN AREAS
CLOSEST TO
THE HOUSE TO
IMPROVE FUNCTION
BUT OTHERWISE
PLANT TO RETAIN
EXISTING LEVELS

STONE WALLS WILL
WITHSTAND THE HARSH
COASTAL ENVIRONMENT
AND ALSO MAKE IT EASY TO
CONSTRUCT CURVES

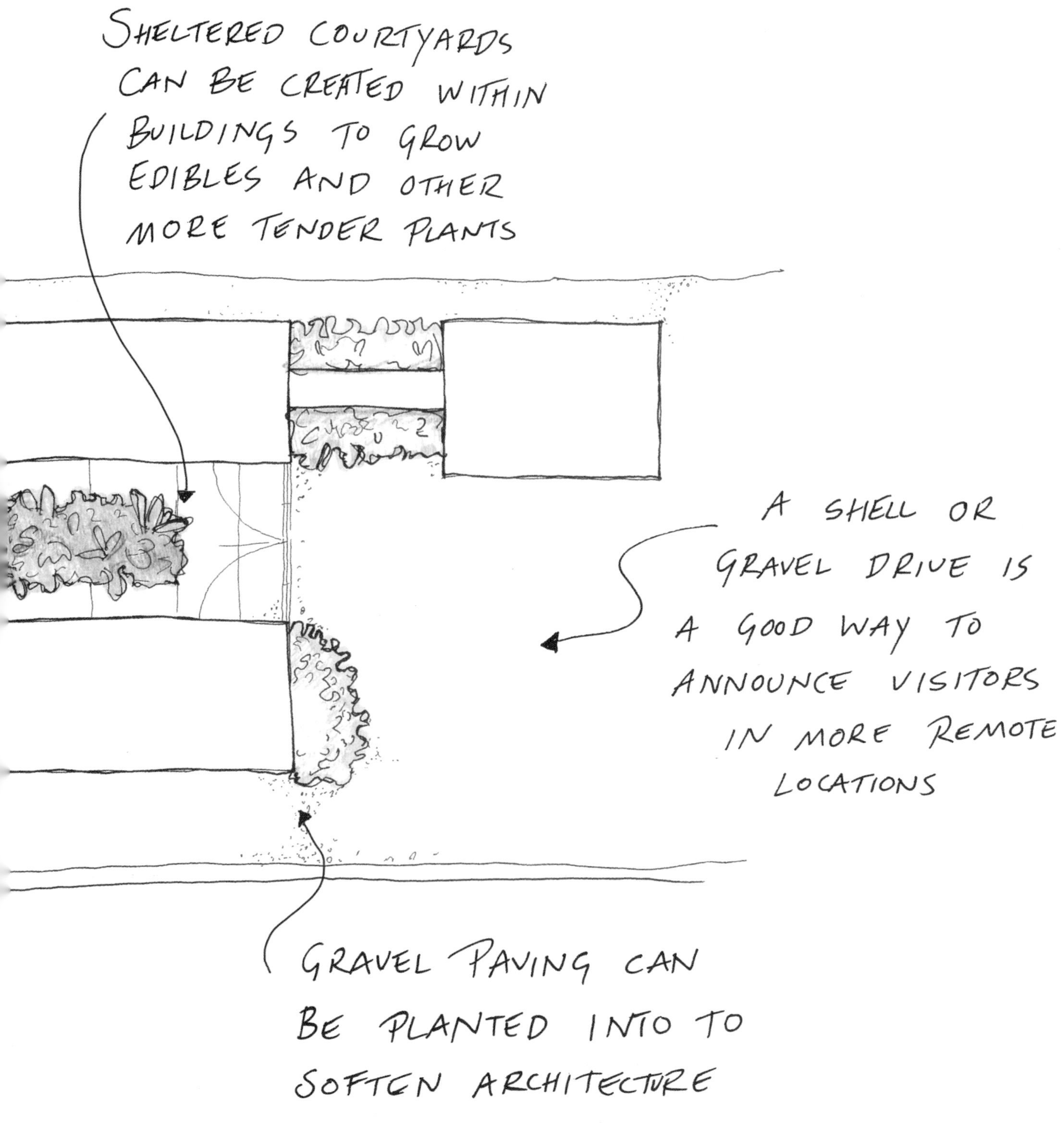

SHELTERED COURTYARDS
CAN BE CREATED WITHIN
BUILDINGS TO GROW
EDIBLES AND OTHER
MORE TENDER PLANTS

A SHELL OR
GRAVEL DRIVE IS
A GOOD WAY TO
ANNOUNCE VISITORS
IN MORE REMOTE
LOCATIONS

GRAVEL PAVING CAN
BE PLANTED INTO TO
SOFTEN ARCHITECTURE

TREES

Leptospermum scoparium
MANUKA

If planted in a windy environment, this simply moulds to the wind. This naturally formed topiary is splendid when in flower.

Knightia excelsa
REWAREWA

This hardy tree has sharp-toothed, leathery leaves and brushlike flowers that will bring birdlife to the garden.

Sophora 'Dragon's gold'
KOWHAI

A popular selection of our beloved kowhai. The yellow flower signalled to Maori that spring had arrived.

Metrosideros excelsa
POHUTUKAWA

Our beloved Christmas tree also makes some of the finest honey.

Rhopalostylis sapida
NIKAU

Great for coastal bush. Beautiful surrounding a beach house and, if established young, very hardy.

Yucca carnerosana
YUCCA

Hardy and easy care. Keep in mind they are not small and are spiky so plant back from buildings and paths.

Corynocarpus laevigatus
KARAKA

These hardy and glossy-leafed trees are great for birds, but the berries are poisonous and children must be taught not to eat them.

SMALL TREES AND SHRUBS

Muehlenbeckia spp.
MUEHLENBECKIA

All three main species are excellent: *M. astonii* is a great mounding shrub, *M. axillaris* a hardy groundcover and *M. complexa* to train up or down walls.

Brachyglottis greyi
RANGIORA, DAISY BUSH

This compact little bush has sunshine-yellow flowers and silver leaves in most situations except shade.

Olearia spp.
OLEARIA

Ideal for hedging in a coastal garden, with wonderful white flowers in spring. *O. cheesemanii* is a great garden plant.

Coprosma robusta or *Coprosma propinqua*
COPROSMA

Berries are attractive to wildlife and an effective weed suppressor.

Echium fastuosum
PRIDE OF MADEIRA

These flowers are quite outstanding . Must have free-draining soil. Ideal for a coastal environment.

Pachystegia spp.
MARLBOROUGH ROCK DAISIES

Beautiful structural leaves are white on the back and waxy green on the front. Flowers, too, are very crisp with a daisy form.

Banksia repens
CREEPING BANKSIA

Just one variety of a larger family suited to tough coastal times. The splendid brush-like flowers are very attractive to both birds and insects.

Clianthus spp.
KAKA BEAK

One of the showier natives. Prone to caterpillars but still well worth growing. Very rare in the wild so good to plant.

GRASSES, REEDS AND FOLIAGE

Astelia banksii
WHARAWHARA

Naturally occurring on the coast in association with pohutukawa, this is a lovely association to recapture.

Desmoschoenus spiralis
PINGAO

An important plant in dune restoration along with *Spinifex* spp. and *Austrofestuca littoralis*. Also much desired for weaving.

Libertia peregrinans
MIKOIKOI

Salt-tolerant and hardy to most conditions except shade, the vibrant orange foliage bears white flowers in spring followed by berries.

FLOWERS

Apodasmia similis
OIOI
Important plant for water filtration. Will tolerate dry periods as well as marginal water zones.

Cortaderia splendens
TOETOE
One of our coastal icons. Great for sweeps of planting in sandy soil that may be vulnerable to erosion.

Beschorneria toneliana
AMOLE
This unusual plant has splendid red flower stems and is as super-hardy as its close relative, agave.

Osteospermum spp.
CAPE DAISY
For a vibrant and wide-ranging source of colour in a harsh environment, this plant with African origins is a standout. Should have full sun.

Arctotis spp.
AFRICAN DAISY
A bright easy scrambler perfect for sandy soils at the beach house.

Felicia amelloides
BLUE MARGUERITE
May look sweet but is happy in a tough coastal garden. Its sky-blue tones look good with a vast horizon out beyond.

Myosotidium hortensia
CHATHAM ISLAND FORGET-ME-NOT, KOPAKOPA
Prefers cooler gardens and thrives in a sheltered south-west position with loads of seaweed in a sandy or gravelly soil.

Celmisia spp.
MOUNTAIN DAISY, TIKUMU
Best suited to cooler gardens. Strikingly architectural form and metallic silver tones, and suprising daisy-like flowers. Beautiful with *Pimelea prostrata*.

Pimelea prostrata
NEW ZEALAND DAPHNE, PINATORO
Unbeatable groundcover in dry, sandy soils.

OTHER PLANTS TO CONSIDER

TREES

Metrosideros umbellata
SOUTHERN RATA

Metrosideros robusta
NORTHERN RATA

Pseudopanax spp.
FIVE FINGER, LANCEWOOD

Dodonaea viscosa
AKEAKE

SMALL TREES AND SHRUBS

Corokia spp.
COROKIA

Carmichaelia spp.
NEW ZEALAND BROOM

Cistus spp.
ROCK ROSE

GRASSES, REEDS AND FOLIAGE

Chionochloa flavicans
DWARF TOETOE

Carex testacea
TUSSOCK

Baumea juncea
JOINTED TWIG RUSH

FLOWERS

Disphyma spp.
NATIVE ICEPLANT

Gazania spp.
GAZANIA

Eschscholzia californica
CALIFORNIA POPPIES

Westringia spp.
WESTRINGIA

Lavandula dentata
LAVENDER

ACCENTS

Agave americana
AGAVE

Yucca rigida
YUCCA

Aloe polyphylla
ALOE

THE NATURAL

Dry
Garden

Gardening was simply not able to happen until we had worked out how to gather and redistribute water. Centuries later irrigation and water transportation has been well mastered but we face new water shortages brought about by increasing populations placing greater and greater strains on our water sources. This competition for water will only increase over time, and even in wet regions we need to consider how we manage this precious resource to best effect. Even regions where water restrictions are not imposed in dry periods face increasing water-supply and wastewater management costs.

THIS IMPOSES NEW CHALLENGES to managing and designing our gardens. We can address them by being judicious about the plants we select, by adopting alternatives to having a lawn, and — most importantly — by more effectively storing and reusing the water that is already running through our gardens.

Every year our roofs collect water that is then expensively transported through our drains and into the sea, along with runoff from the roads. This water can be effectively and more cleanly processed through our gardens. Household bath and shower water, washing machine runoff and non-greasy dishwater is completely harmless to our gardens and can be a valuable source of water in times when restrictions are in place.

The technology to manage this under-utilised water is well developed and the economic and environmental savings are well documented. The only barrier is the costs of the initial outlay. The advantage, though, is not just the ongoing reduction in the water bill but also the freedom to grow a wider range of plant material, particularly food crops — which offers another economic incentive.

Once you have assessed how you can more effectively use the water you have, be it through recycling household water, measuring and metering what you use in the garden or simply storing rainwater for outdoor use, you need to consider how best you are going to use this water in your outdoor spaces.

The design of your garden has a significant impact on how much water is needed to maintain a healthy living space. Large areas without green cover lose water at a faster rate; plants are in fact the most effective means of retaining water. In Dubai gardens are planted very densely; the sooner a complete cover of green is established, the more quickly the transpiration from the ground plummets.

Lawns, however, are thirsty beasts. If you think of the quantity of lawn clippings that you can pile up in a summer and its weight in

◄ **LEFT** A dry garden such as a coastal one does not need to be spiky to do well when water is restricted. Silver and grey tones are often an indication that plants are suited to hot and dry conditions. Globe artichokes, blueberries and silver thyme are all suitable productive plants. Himalayan white birches have stunning paper-white bark that works well with these sorts of tones.

water, it will give you some idea of the water you are wasting with a traditional lawn. Plastic lawns look increasingly pleasing but in my view they're not an adequate alternative. They are not 'alive' and so they don't contribute at all to cooling a space. Sure they don't reflect as much heat as concrete but nor do they absorb it. They also process no carbon dioxide so they should be considered as a paving medium rather than as part of the green belt in a garden.

There are, however, a wide range of ground covers, both native and otherwise, that provide a flat usable area without requiring constant cutting. Their advantage is they don't need to be replenishing growth constantly through a dry period to maintain a good appearance.

However, if a lawn is a must then the planning could be as simple as considering how large it really needs to be. If you think each square metre will happily soak up a litre of water on a summer's day, then it's clear that significant savings can be made by reducing the scale of a lawn area. You can also reduce water loss by creating a canopy of trees above, although in very dry periods, when the water table is low, the trees are likely to out-compete a lawn for any available water with their more efficient root systems.

A DRY GARDEN does not need to resemble a desert, and the gardens of hot-climate regions such as Spain, Africa and the Middle East make that perfectly apparent. I was once fortunate to visit the ruins of an old palace garden in Morocco. The walls and floors of the ruins had long since been stripped of their beautiful tiles but the irrigation system and water features were, even in the heat of the summer, still running a shallow source of water. Four sunken citrus groves were a beautiful fresh green and covered in fruit. Because the tiles had been removed we could see the complex system of rills that had been frugally but effectively directing water to the orchard over the hundreds of years since anyone had occupied the palace.

Rather than a garden being a dry and barren place, closed rooms can become sensual sanctuaries from a harsh environment. Colour, fragrance and water are all carefully embraced as essential elements in a garden. Efficiency is paramount, though. Where water is scarce, not a drop should be wasted nor used but once. Sunken gardens below an outdoor living court, for example, can receive all the run-off from patios and rooftops. In Japanese gardens, roof water is run down chains and into clay pipes to be distributed most efficiently. Water plays a critical role in cooling living spaces and a water feature in a dry garden will have great effect.

When a garden is young and establishing, it is a very tough place for plants. The trees and shrubs with strong and complex root systems that will make their way deep into water tables, drawing moisture efficiently from the soil, have yet to develop. That's why in areas prone to drought you should always plant in autumn, giving plants a full cycle of the wet season, such as it is, to strengthen and develop an effective root system before the dry weather comes. Many plants that might seem unsuited to dry areas can in fact weather a drought if they have been given such a good start.

> The great joy of a dry garden is that even in the most restrictive areas where your choice is limited to just drought-tolerant species you needn't settle for the mundane.

UNLESS YOU ARE happy to hand-water with recycled water from baths or the washing up, pots and planters are best limited as these will always dry out first. Use them instead to grow a few soft herbs and lettuces on a sheltered balcony out of a hot summer's sun and away from the competition in your main beds. But you will still need to hand-water every day.

The great joy of a dry garden is that even in the most restrictive areas where your choice is limited to just drought-tolerant species you needn't settle for the mundane. Most drought-tolerant species occupy landscapes such as deserts where they are required to be bold and bright in order to attract the insects or birds upon which they depend

for pollination. The flowers of leucospermum, kangaroo paws, poppies and brilliantly spired echium all compete for attention with vibrant blooms set upon silvery or leathery foliage. This foliage, too, is designed to help the plant survive as it protects the plants from the harsh light. The fat leaves of succulents are adept at water storage, sustaining them through periods of drought. Even the spikes common in desert cactus are a record of the plant's arid origins: a plant that needs to withstand months or even years without rain cannot afford to lose a single leaf to a passing marauder as this last leaf could mean the difference between surviving until the next rain falls.

Whether the garden you create reflects its arid nature through your choice of well-suited plant material or hides its true nature by using limited resources to the best effect, the results are sure to be more interesting than your average quarter-acre with lawn.

Design Guide

WATER STORAGE

THE MODERN TANK has come a long way since the large concrete water tower that stood on a hill. Now a water tank can be effectively placed in any cavity that can be accessed. Modular units are able to be built into freestanding walls, creating a water tank that doubles as screening. Bladder systems can be stored under decks or in basements and will mould into even quite awkward areas. They also have the advantage of being easily installed into existing gaps where access may be quite limited; like any inflatable they are very small until filled with water. A water tank can even double as a water feature in periods of wet, with an overflow that becomes a fountain spilling into garden beds. The limits are only what you can imagine.

While tanks can be retrofitted, it is most efficient if they are

► **RIGHT** This hardy-native planting in a Queenstown garden by Ralf Krüger includes common plants such as pittosporum, flax and carex, brought to life with a drift of delphiniums. Flowers do not need to be overabundant to add to the value of a garden nor should they be kept separate from native plants in a suburban setting.

included in the design of the garden right from the start, integrated to make the most efficient use of space and placed where they are of most use to the gardener. Ideally they'd be positioned to ensure a good head of water so a pump is not required to run the tap. You also need to decide what water you are planning to store and whether you wish the water to be of drinking quality or if it is just needed for gardening and other outdoor activities such as washing a car. Much of our wastewater such as grey water is great for the garden. However, if you are storing grey water it's advisable to have a tap that can redirect it into a traditional wastewater system for the occasions where you may be using harder chemicals or washing greasy dishes with animal fats that could cause the water to turn toxic or poisonous.

You also need to be aware that this water is not drinkable quality so councils will not accept it being attached to outdoor showers. It can, however, be used for flushing toilets, which is another surprisingly large proportion of our water use. If you are collecting off the roof then your water will be cleaner as long as your roof is suited for water collection (that is, it's not made of a chemically reactive or toxic material such as asbestos). The limit to this, though, is that if there has been no rain then you will be running low on your tank supply, too. In the perfect world two tanks could be installed to manage the separate systems and you could effectively be collecting and using your water twice.

DISTRIBUTION

IT IS REALLY important that water is not wasted. Irrigation systems can be more bother than they are worth in an area with high rainfall, where a garden grows so fast that it is constantly changing and pipes are used for such a short period of the year that they are likely to have been damaged by a garden fork in the months in between use. In a dry garden, however, irrigation is essential and the timing of watering is also critical.

◄ **LEFT** Mimicking nature, especially water, is never as easy as it appears but we can learn a lot through observation. A stony water feature, here by Ralf Krüger, should include large rocks as well as smaller stones and polished river pebbles. Ideally these should be all from the same source of stone so they appear to have been 'processed' on site.

WATER FEATURES

IT MAY SEEM a luxury to have a water feature when water is scarce but in fact a water feature is not only very soothing in a hot climate, it can also be integrated into the design of the garden as part of an efficient water distribution system, or as an overflow of water storage or even a back-up water storage unit itself. In Australia, where gardeners face the challenges of water shortage and also the risk of fire, natural swimming pools have been designed to double as a supply of water in the event of fire. Pumps triggered by smoke will drench the house in pool water.

HARD SURFACES

WHILE PERMEABLE SURFACES that allow free flow of water through them are considered desirable in most gardens because they ensure that most of the rainfall replenishes the water table, in a garden on water restrictions hard surfaces can also work well if they are used to collect water and redirect it to the areas where it is most needed. This could be as simple as making sure the garden is below the patio and that the gradient of the patio slopes slightly in the desired direction. Having the garden slightly lower is even more desirable in an area which has extremes of wet and dry; flooding can be as much of a problem as drought at the opposite end of a season.

SHADE

THERE IS NO better way to stop water loss than a canopy of green. Establishing trees that will shade the ground below, especially in a hard courtyard, will have more of an impact on the temperature below than most shade sails or canopies. Alternatively, climbing a grape or passionfruit over a pergola can do a lot to create a cool ambience and retain water beneath.

► **RIGHT** Steps could have been used here but instead Ralf Krüger has formed a path out of slabs of schist moulded to the form of the landscape, creating a strong sense of perspective that pulls you up the hill comfortably.

WATER VALUES

IF WATER IS at a premium you need to consider creating a set of water values for the different areas of your garden. This is essentially planning different zones of watering into the design. Depending on your family's requirements, a vegetable garden may be your highest priority and this would be your zone one. These are the plantings that would be watered first and most frequently, even in times of drought. A lawn, on the other hand, is normally the first to be abandoned and would be a zone ten, the last to be watered. Trees and shrubs would be somewhere in the middle, say zones five and six, as although their water requirements are not as great, the value of having to replace a mature tree is greater. Considering these water values as you plan the garden can help you put a realistic plan in place and should allow you to estimate what sort of water consumption you require in extreme circumstances, and how well your garden is likely to fare.

COURTYARDS

THE COURTYARD GARDEN with sunken beds and a central water feature has to be mentioned in a section on dry gardens. The tradition of a cool outdoor courtyard space, often at the centre of a house, originated in the hotter regions of the world. They were sanctuaries from the hot sun and they were as much outdoor rooms as they were gardens, integral to the design of a house.

These outdoor rooms, however, were not without plants. The fragrance of flowers was critical and fruiting trees such as citrus were also highly desirable, both for fruit and the scent of their blossoms. Tiles and formwork were generally intricate and often brightly coloured, just as in an interior room. It was, and is, a complete canvas that maintained its own symmetry. With limited space for planting, each chosen plant serves a function — be it productive or purely sensual.

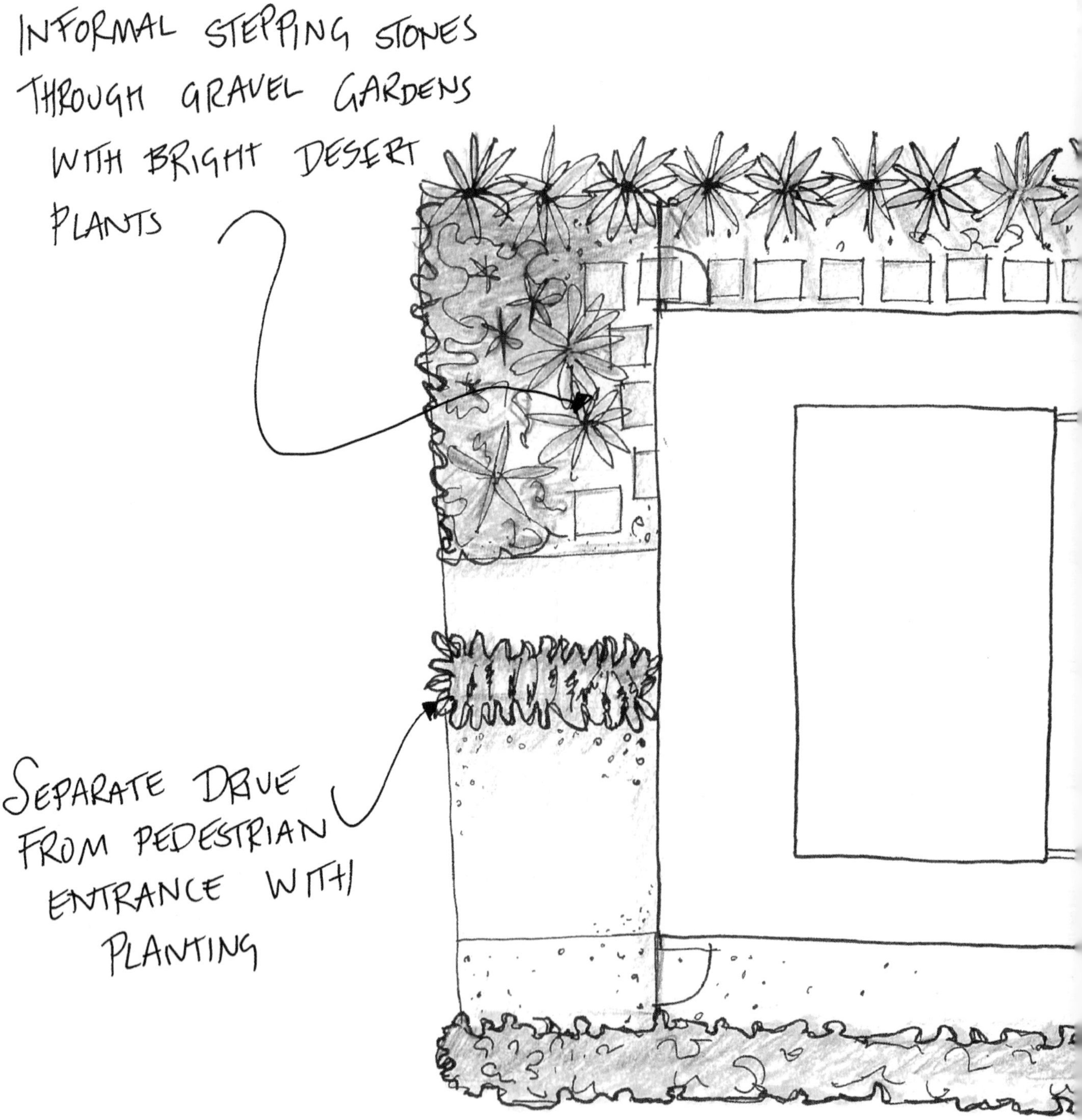

INFORMAL STEPPING STONES
THROUGH GRAVEL GARDENS
WITH BRIGHT DESERT
PLANTS

SEPARATE DRIVE
FROM PEDESTRIAN
ENTRANCE WITH
PLANTING

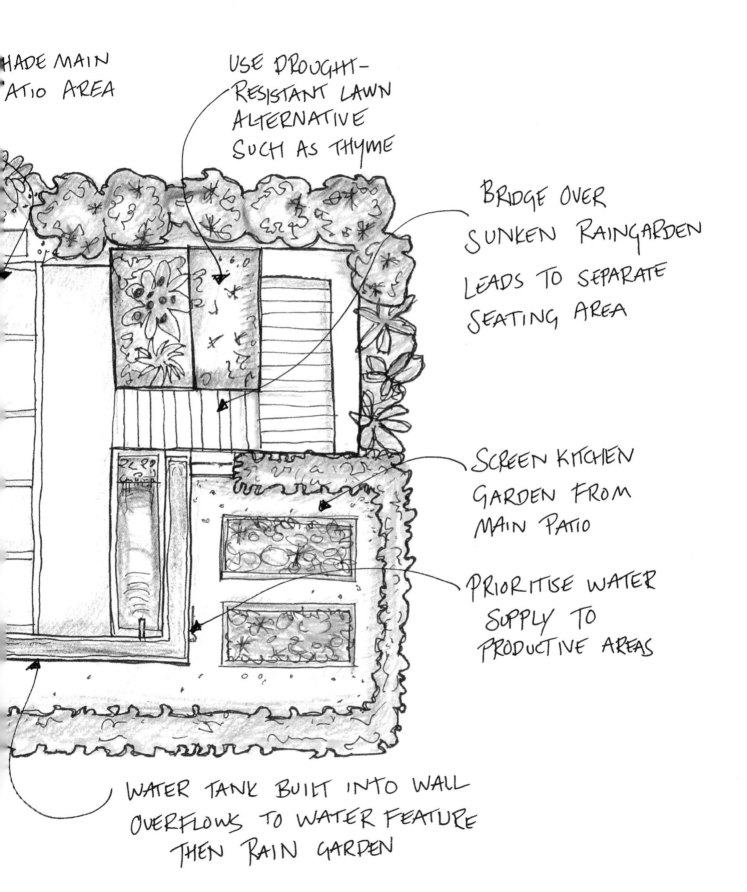

HADE MAIN
ATIO AREA

USE DROUGHT-
RESISTANT LAWN
ALTERNATIVE
SUCH AS THYME

BRIDGE OVER
SUNKEN RAINGARDEN
LEADS TO SEPARATE
SEATING AREA

SCREEN KITCHEN
GARDEN FROM
MAIN PATIO

PRIORITISE WATER
SUPPLY TO
PRODUCTIVE AREAS

WATER TANK BUILT INTO WALL
OVERFLOWS TO WATER FEATURE
THEN RAIN GARDEN

Salvia leucantha
MEXICAN BUSH SAGE

Grows to around one metre tall.
Loves the heat and resents
overwatering, making it perfect
for a harsher dry environment.

Pimelea prostratus
NATIVE DAPHNE, PINATORO

With silver-toned small, fine-toothed
leaves and a carpet of white star flowers,
this groundcover is both hardy and
delightful. Has a gentle fragrance.

Rosmarinus prostratus
ROSEMARY

This aromatic herb is so versatile from
full sun to dappled shade.

Thymus spp.
THYME

This groundcover will happily scramble
through stony soils. Be careful about
planting in some areas of the South
Island where some species are pests.

Helenium spp.
HELENIUM

Flowering with sunset colours
from late summer well into autumn.
Great in a border or drifting through
a gravel garden.

Verbascum thapsus
VERBASCUM

As well as beautiful spires of flowers the
fluffy silver leaves indicate this plant's
resilience to tough climates. Start from
seed or mature plant.

Felicia amelloides
BLUE MARGUERITE

This blue-petalled daisy may look sweet
but it is happy in a tough dry garden.

Hylotelephium telephium
AUTUMN SEDUM

This perennial brings colour and form
to the garden in late autumn when little
else is up and about. It is also a great
plant for bees at this time of year.

Osteospermum spp.
CAPE DAISY

For a vibrant and wide-ranging source
of colour in a harsh environment,
this plant with African origins is a
standout. Should have full sun.

Lavandula spp.
LAVENDER
Resilience to dry conditions makes lavender a great plant for an arid garden, especially if you're looking for some colour that will look after itself.

Cotyledon orbiculata
COTYLEDON
Like other succulents such as *Echeveria* spp., *Crassula* spp. and *Kalanchoe* spp., this is great for dry gardens. Be careful in coastal regions where it may be invasive.

Carmichaelia spp.
NATIVE BROOM
Our native brooms are endangered in their natural habitat but are stunning garden plants with a form like earthen seaweed.

Phormium cookianum
MOUNTAIN FLAX
Suited to many smaller gardens as it is more compact than *P. tenax*. Its flowers also vary, with attractive yellow stems.

Agave attenuata
AGAVE
Agave shelter snails. The snails don't so much enjoy eating them as taking cover beneath the leaves. A good place to look if you have other plants under attack.

Aloe plicatilis
ALOE
Unusually formed, this hardy plant will turn a splendid red in dry seasons. This is actually a sign of stress so if the red doesn't abate, add water and a liquid feed.

Salvia 'Blue Hills'
SALVIA
This is one of the most reliable free-flowering salvias, with solid blocks of deep purple lasting through summer and well into the end of autumn.

Anigozanthos spp.
KANGAROO PAWS
This is my favourite Australian plant. Simple swordlike foliage bears furry and fancifully formed flowers in hot orange, red, yellow and green.

Armeria maritima
THRIFT
This fine grass-like leaved groundcover bears pink or white pompom flowers throughout summer and well into autumn. Prefers good drainage.

Argyranthemum frutescens
MARGUERITE DAISY
This family of daisies offers a broad colour palette and they are easy-care cheerful garden plants.

Euphorbia glauca
NATIVE EUPHORBIA
Our only native euphorbia, this delicate blue perennial is a wonderful highlight and well adapted to such conditions.

Hemerocallis spp.
DAYLILY
Though the foliage is not particularly impressive, the daylily is a hardy and reliable perennial. A vast range of colours to suit most tastes.

Agave geminiflora
AGAVE
A really interesting agave with a spiralling form of long, pointed dark-green leaves with white frays.

Pachystegia spp.
MARLBOROUGH ROCK DAISY
Has beautiful structural leaves that are white on the back and waxy green on the front. The flowers, too, are very crisp and structural and have a daisy form.

TREES AND SHRUBS

Telopea truncata
WARATAH
This Australian family of trees is tricky to grow in a normal garden setting, preferring stony soils and low nutrients to pampering and rich humus.

Leucospermum spp.
PINCUSHION PROTEA
These stand-out flowers are like iridescent fireworks. Must have free-draining soil and are intolerant of clay but otherwise hardy.

Yucca spp.
YUCCA
Come in a range of shapes and sizes and are popular for their architectural form as well as hardiness. Also have splendid flowers when mature.

Strelitzia spp.
BIRD OF PARADISE
Most common is the shrub *S. reginae*; lesser known forms to consider are *S. nicolai*, which fans six metres high, and *S. juncea*, which has elegantly formed leaves.

Aloe spp.
ALOE

This family contains the plants *A. vera* and *A. arborescens*, highly valued for their medicinal attributes. Also provide colour and food for birds through the winter.

Aloe thraskii
ALOE

These amazing trees with trunks like elephant legs look like they have stepped out of a Doctor Seuss book.

Banksia repens
CREEPING BANKSIA

Just one variety of a larger family suited to tough dry climes. The splendid brush-like flowers are very attractive to birds and insects alike.

Grevillea spp.
GREVILLEA

The grevillea has adapted to handle the heat and harshness of the Australian climate. Treat it tough.

OTHER PLANTS TO CONSIDER

FLOWERS AND TEXTURE

Lithodora 'Grace Ward'
LITHODORA

Phlomis fruticosa
JERUSALEM SAGE

Convolvulus cneorum
SILVER BUSH

Cerastium tomentosum
SNOW IN SUMMER

Festuca coxii
COX'S FESCUE

Echeveria spp.
HEN AND CHICKEN FERN

TREES AND SHRUBS

Callistemon spp.
BOTTLEBRUSH

Dracaena draco
DRAGON TREE

Echium spp.
PRIDE OF MADEIRA

Cistus spp.
ROCK ROSE

Corokia 'Dark Spire'
COROKIA

Leucadendron spp.
CONE BUSH

THE NATURAL
Country
Garden

If a garden were a manuscript, the urban garden would be a short story and the country garden a novel. To perfect a small garden is one thing but to reach that same level of detail on such a large canvas requires absolute commitment. The limitlessness of a large piece of land can be absolutely overwhelming. Of course there's the inherent appeal of being able to take what had been paddocks and turning them into a garden but it's certainly not a one-step process.

▲ **PREVIOUS PAGES** Two of my favourite native grasses, *Anemanthele lessoniana* and *Chionochloa flavicans* are punctuated by informal pillars in this Ralf Krüger garden, a pleasing collision between soft simple brushstrokes and structure.

Maples at Tamata nurseries in a blaze of autumn colour. In a country garden you have the space to make dramatic plantings such as this.

► **RIGHT** The bigger your space the more in control of the journey you should be. If you want to turn the viewer to announce a view you can emphasise this not just by kinking the path but also by shifting from a simple strong drift of planting to a punctuation mark, as this Piet Ouldolf garden shows.

IN A SUBURBAN environment our boundaries are clear; in the country our boundaries are best left undefined. Everything moves at a different pace. In a city garden a driveway is just about function but in the country it becomes an opportunity for an experience: the sound of car wheels crunching on the gravel driveway, an avenue of trees that wrap around you as you curve towards the house.

The well-cultivated gardens that hug the country house show the owner's strong relationship to the land and a masterful ability to tame it. Beyond these borders, the master gardener begins a slow unravelling of this tamed nature as it unfolds into the landscape beyond.

Managing the transition between these two scales is the first boundary in a country garden. This is why traditional estate gardens often began with a central axis and a series of rooms or closed spaces with different purposes and intents: from the kitchen garden and the orchard, to the herb garden and the glasshouse, the organisation of a garden into intended spaces is an excellent starting point. Deciding first upon the function and then upon the arrangement is the best way to discipline what could otherwise become an unruly beast.

> The well-cultivated gardens that hug the country house show the owner's strong relationship to the land and a masterful ability to tame it.

It is critical to plan the garden in its entirety so you have a sense of the relationships between different spaces, but it's also important not to start too many projects at once. One at a time from start to finish should be the rule. The most intense period of a garden is as it establishes, and this is enough for most people to focus on in one go. If you push too hard with too many areas at once you will miss the opportunity to complete details and to finely tune a garden as you plant.

YOU ALSO NEED to understand that most gardens will never be static. Quite often our ambitions may need one, two or even three generations

of planting before they can be realised. You cannot have a shade garden until trees have matured and offer shade; you won't have reflections in your pond until it is surrounded by layers of planting; and you should not expect an orchard to be productive without time for it to mature.

It's this long-term vision that makes the country garden unique. It requires a relationship with a piece of land that can last a lifetime, or even generations. At no time does the garden ever look quite the same and with every new gardener, regardless of their declaration that they will follow the original plans, come new brushstrokes. Nature, too, has its influence, with storms and floods and dry summers all playing their part in determining the garden's changing shape.

But, oh, what a journey: to plant a tree that will outlive you, and to look out over a vista that once was a paddock and to remember every seed that was sown, every tree that was planted. Buried amongst it all is a lifetime of memories.

The magic is always in the detail, but for a large garden to be manageable — especially if you aspire to high standards — the detail must be concentrated into deliberate moments. Too much fuss is actually less pleasurable; we need moments of simplicity and movement and also moments in which to stand still for a garden on this scale to feel like a complete experience.

A kitchen garden is an industrious space and needs wide clean paths through which we can move with a wheelbarrow, while a cut-flower garden is more a place to muse and is more inclined to have gentle paths that amble. A bush walk is most effective with just a simple track, while your main entertaining area needs to have clear paths that are hard wearing. It's important to focus on these practicalities before you get carried away with a grand design. If function is not served then even the most delightful concepts can feel slightly uncomfortable, even though you may not be quite able to work out why.

SCALE IS BOTH a challenge and a liberation. While the vastness can be overwhelming, there is suddenly a range of trees that are completely

inappropriate for most home gardens but here can be planted en masse. I am still inclined to keep larger trees back from the house and to increase the size of specimens as the planting itself increases in scale. Not only do the larger sweeps of planting and trees scale well in the distant garden but as your garden plan gets further and further from the domestic zone around the house, the planting needs to become simpler. After all, it's moving further from any irrigation system, and also from the eyes of the gardener. The more labour-intensive a section of garden is, the closer it should be to the house both so hard work gets the most appreciation from visitors — and so it gets done first!

The more natural your plantings become as they drift further out into the landscape, the better, too. If you imagine a piece of knitting slowly unravelling into the horizon beyond, you are on the right track.

The garden will be better discovered if each of its sections leads you from one to the next. Be it by full disclosure or through a tease of colour through a garden wall, you want the viewer to continually be asking the question, what is behind there? And answering it with a sigh of unexpected pleasure as they turn the corner.

Design guide

THE VISTA

WHEN WE HAVE THE SCOPE to do so, and a property that justifies having a ride-on mower, it's hard to resist a long sweeping vista from the house to the countryside beyond. It's like the reverse of a picture frame, an open expanse that encourages the eye to look beyond and afar. Traditionally a vista would be a flat rectangular lawn with trees or hedge rows either side, but there is no reason why a vista cannot wind out like a curling river. The intention of a vista is to extend the perspective, not to foreshorten, so the edges of the form should stretch

into the landscape rather than enclose it. Essentially the length should be at least twice, and ideally three times, greater than the width.

THE GARDEN ROOM

IT'S IMPORTANT to engage with the landscape, but also to provide refuge from it by offering intimate spaces on a more human scale. If you have the scope you can provide a range of different spaces that create different moods. A seat that we enjoy sitting on alone or with one other can be quite different from a seating area where we would gather with a group of friends. People like corners where they are sheltered behind but can look out over, or into, an attractive scene. Garden rooms are even more powerful when they contrast with the surrounding landscape.

Corridors, too, can be used to interesting effect, leading people in and out of gardens. Walls on this scale are most effectively created with hedges. The larger the garden, the further a budget needs to stretch and even the cheapest fencing can't compete for value with a hedge. Sure you have to trim them but hedge trimmers these days are fantastic beasts. My husband and I are always a bit disappointed when the other gets to the hedges first, such is the enjoyment, but on a larger property there is sure to be plenty of trimming to share around.

THE LAKE

IF YOU ARE lucky enough to have a swampland on your property, it makes far more sense to transform it into a lake than to attempt to drain it. If this is your privilege, consider an island with a bridge. Not only does an island create another destination but it also creates a sense of depth, a reason to walk around the lake and see what is on the other side. A bridge, too, is a wonderful opportunity for a composition and you should think not just of the bridge itself but also how its mirrored

► **RIGHT** This bridge at Dalton's sits over 'a valley of bulbs' planted through ordinary grass that is never mown. Constructed out of macrocarpa slabs balanced on large river boulders, this could be replicated in any garden. The transition from a lawn path to a hard surface gives the voyeur a reason to stop and contemplate. The yellow blooms are the common gladioli.

image reflected in the water completes the composition.

Consider, too, a range of depths within the lake for different types of aquatic and marginal plants. Plants are important, not just to add to the charm but also to keep water quality clear. If you have effective plantings, you will be able to use the lake to process stormwater on your property before it flows off into rivers or streams. Consider also whether you wish to use a lake for rowing around. If you do, you need to consider the depth and ensure you have appropriately sized channels for your desired vessel. A bridge also needs to allow room for you to float beneath on a summer's afternoon. If stuck for inspiration take a look at the painter Monet's garden and you'll be away.

When you plant the banks with trees think about reflections, and imagine them leaning across the pond and petals falling on the lake surface. These are the magical moments that reward toil.

PATHS

ONE OF THE PLEASURES of being in the country is getting off the road, onto the beaten track and into more sensible shoes. While certain areas like a patio or a potage may suit sturdier paths, the further we get from the house, the more informal a path can become. Lawn paths are very inviting, stepping stones have intrigue, and gravel paths create a beautiful fresh contrast to overflowing beds. Consider, too, rammed earth — but not if you are in an area of high rainfall. Lime chip will give you the brightest look and works well with dark green plantings and strong form or colour.

ARRIVING

IF YOU HAVE the space, arriving home should be a reward that gets the space it deserves. Be it a winding tree-clad drive, a tunnel of bush lined with arching mamaku or a breathtaking view of the beyond, an

entrance should be designed to be an event. This is one of the moments when simplicity is the best response. When we are in our cars we do not need a lot of detail and instead bold is best. Decide whether you want to reveal the house at the gate or hide it until you reach the end of a tunnel of trees. Sometimes a sneak teaser will work well, just a flicker before the great arrival. Whether your house is a sweet cottage or something more stately, its character should be intensified by the arrival experience.

FOLLIES

I FIRST FELL IN LOVE with follies reading Agatha Christie; her stories often had a body or an undisclosed meeting turning up in a folly of sorts on a grand estate. Traditionally a folly is a building within the landscape which is essentially a faux house. Quite often they were small replicas of exotic architecture, a record of another civilisation. Traditionally follies were quite literally interpreted, but you can be as abstract as you like. Imagine small pyramids in a field, a replica of Stonehenge, or a replica of a bunker such as those found on Auckland's Bastion Point. In more recent times the sculpture park has, in many ways, taken the place of the folly; instead of miniature buildings all sorts of playful forms dance on and with the lay of the land.

If you want to create a folly, consider how it will be discovered. Ideally you want sneak views across a lake or through trees so there is a sense of enquiry and discovery. It is ideally placed in a spot that you think is particularly beautiful and that you wish to draw people to, for a sunset, a view, or the best of the day's sun. A folly is most fun if you can engage with it in some way, be it climbing, sitting or looking through. If it offers shelter it can be used for picnics or a child's play space as well. Also consider lighting; it can add to a narrative and make the most of something playful. After all, every now and then it is okay for function to follow form.

HILLS AND CONTOURS

IDEALLY A GARDEN should follow the landscape. Like a well-tailored dress that emphasis the best curves and covers those less desirable bumps, so can plantings smooth out the rougher aspects of a landscape. Around the house you may wish to flatten some areas, or if the landscape is very flat there is great advantage in creating contours of your own. Creating hollows can lead to lovely microclimates which will allow you to grow a range of different things that otherwise may be challenging. It also creates a complete contrast to a level plane.

If you are surrounded by hills and valleys, or look on them in the distance, take time to study the form of the landscape beyond before you make any changes. Decide whether you wish to mimic its rolls or crevices or whether you wish to contrast it with crisp lines that show control in your immediate domain. Both can be done to dramatic effect, but to ignore your surroundings entirely is to miss an opportunity. Giving your garden a sense of place and tying it to the unique characteristics of a region, as well as to the more obvious cues of house and pasture, strengthen its character and cultural value.

COLOURS

EVERY REGION has its own palette of colour. Consider this when planning your garden and take cues from the colours beyond. Colour in a garden is like a living canvas that shifts with every season; synchronising it is like conducting an orchestra. If you can manage to tune into the composition beyond your borders, you have a symphony.

It is important to understand cool and warm colours and the effect they have. Reds and warm colours jump forward, while blues and whites expand a horizon. Drop touches of yellow into a blue border — even just occasional drifts and drops — and its warmth will gently help to pull your eye through the plantings as well as providing contrast. Drop touches of deep purple into a rich red border, and as well as

sharp contrast you will anchor the plantings in the same way a shadow anchors an object to the ground.

If you wish to drift from one colour to the next, don't jump around freely but blend from one colour, weaving the plantings together so the transition is part of the composition. It also helps to drop a touch of an earlier colour into a composition again in places to help us connect a garden all together.

You can also use what I call 'memory plants' to connect the changing plantings. They are simple plants of texture that will link through very different plantings, allowing you to shift from one thing to the next without doing so too abruptly. Even though they may not be noticed, they help to ease transition. In most of my gardens I have a theme plant such as a grass or a groundcover that links such vastly different gardens as flower beds and native bush. In a large garden you can afford to have a few of these, sometimes using one or two and perhaps once allowing them all to come together.

NAMING

THOUGH SOME may think it quaint or pretentious, a garden — especially a significant garden in the country — deserves a name. After all, it is a lifetime's work, as well as a home, and it should be named, if only for history's sake.

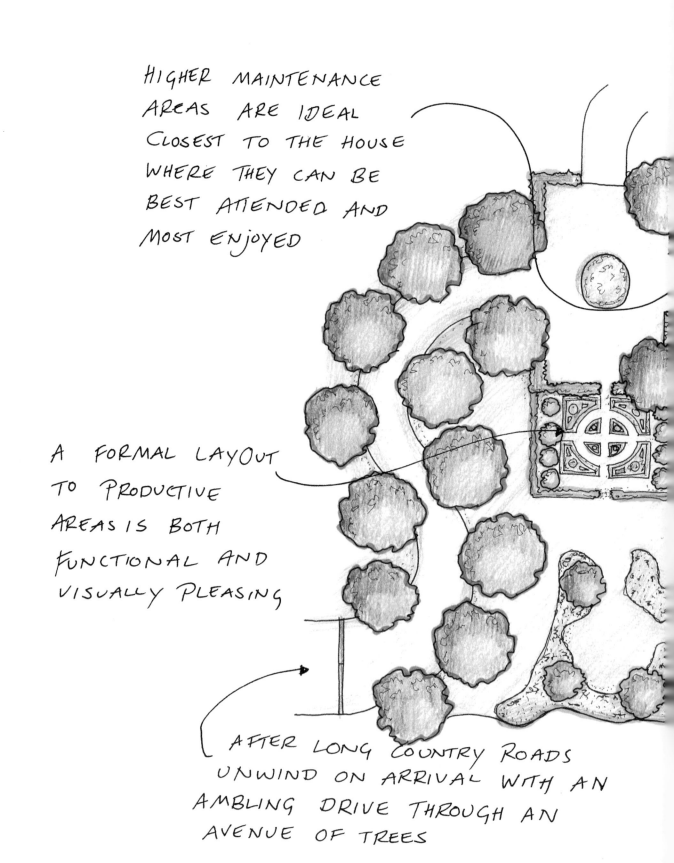

HIGHER MAINTENANCE AREAS ARE IDEAL CLOSEST TO THE HOUSE WHERE THEY CAN BE BEST ATTENDED AND MOST ENJOYED

A FORMAL LAYOUT TO PRODUCTIVE AREAS IS BOTH FUNCTIONAL AND VISUALLY PLEASING

AFTER LONG COUNTRY ROADS UNWIND ON ARRIVAL WITH AN AMBLING DRIVE THROUGH AN AVENUE OF TREES

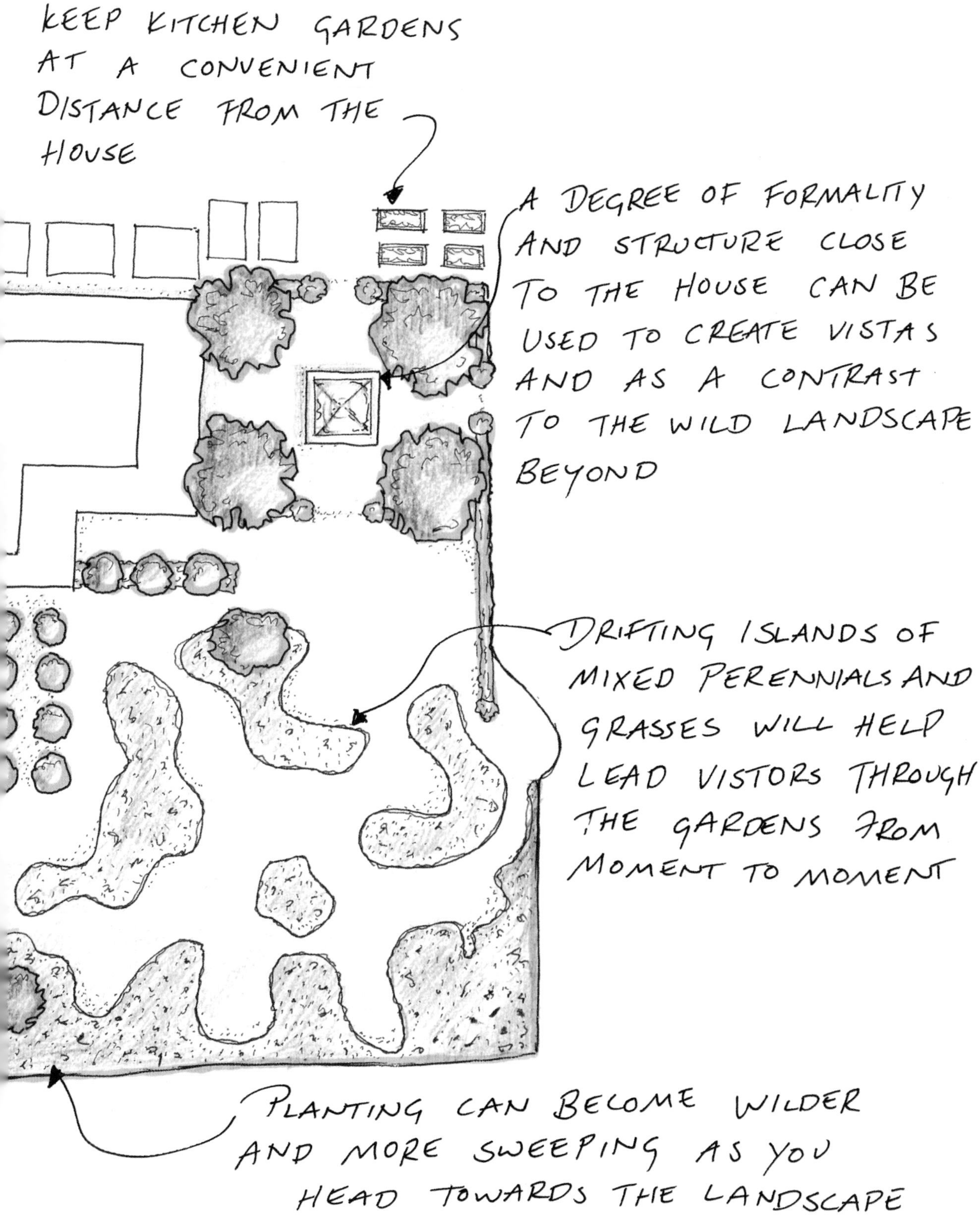

KEEP KITCHEN GARDENS
AT A CONVENIENT
DISTANCE FROM THE
HOUSE

A DEGREE OF FORMALITY
AND STRUCTURE CLOSE
TO THE HOUSE CAN BE
USED TO CREATE VISTAS
AND AS A CONTRAST
TO THE WILD LANDSCAPE
BEYOND

DRIFTING ISLANDS OF
MIXED PERENNIALS AND
GRASSES WILL HELP
LEAD VISTORS THROUGH
THE GARDENS FROM
MOMENT TO MOMENT

PLANTING CAN BECOME WILDER
AND MORE SWEEPING AS YOU
HEAD TOWARDS THE LANDSCAPE

TREES

Magnolia spp.
MAGNOLIA

A must-have. Many special varieties bred here and grown all over the world, ranging from flowers the size of dinner plates to tight, neat blooms.

Betula utilis subsp. *jacquemontii*
HIMALAYAN WHITE BIRCH

The paper-white bark makes this a very special and attractive landscape tree. In winter the bare trunks can be used to great effect.

Prunus spp.
CHERRY TREE

While irresistible in a flower garden, in a large garden planted en masse these are utterly romantic.

Rhododendron spp.
RHODODENDRON

Ideal for volcanic soils. Likes the south side of a hill and shelter from winds.

Malus 'Wright's Scarlet'
CRAB APPLE

Simple and splendid when in fruit. A nice smaller tree to plant closer to buildings.

Leptospermum spp.
MANUKA

Sometimes overlooked as a garden plant, yet it is splendid for borders and creeping varieties make colourful groundcover.

Calliandra spp.
CALLIANDRA

This delightful small tree carries fairy-tale pompoms in autumn. Planted alongside maples and hydrangeas, the antique tones are sublime.

Acer palmatum
JAPANESE MAPLE

There is good reason this is so highly valued in Japanese design. Planted in groves, no other tree creates such magic when light plays through its leaves.

SHRUBS

Hibiscus syriacus
HIBISCUS

This deciduous hibiscus is a sweet addition to the fringes of a woodland planting.

Hydrangea spp.
HYDRANGEA

Good in borders and also easily propagated to bulk up numbers and plant along unsightly fence lines.

Michelia spp.
MICHELIA

A wonderful flowering and fragrant hedge or large standard. Though not quick to establish, the long-term results are worth the wait.

Daphne odora
DAPHNE

This small shrub is a garden delight. Needs a sheltered spot, ideally with morning sun and rich, free-draining soil and on the edge of a dripline or eaves.

Camellia spp.
CAMELLIA

In a country garden you have the opportunity to select large species and let them grow to maturity. *C. japonica* are really best at this scale.

Azalea spp.
AZALEA

Compact and small, and closely related to rhododendrons. Attractive if kept clipped.

Protea spp.
PROTEA

Great for a hot clay bank, these South African beauties enjoy less fertile soils.

HARDY PERENNIALS

Nymphaea alba
WATER LILY

If you have an artificial lake why not cover it in water lilies? Avoid waterways that connect to natural streams and rivers.

Iris spp.
IRIS

Wonderful planted in drifts through grasses or around a pond. Vast range of colours to choose from.

Dahlia spp.
DAHLIA

There are many New Zealand-bred varieties of dahlia. Larger gardens may have space for tree dahlias, which can grow up to three metres tall.

Hemerocallis
DAYLILY
For large garden beds these are such a reliable plant. Plant in sweeps or drifts with colours to match surrounding plantings.

Rosa spp.
ROSE
There is a rose for every garden. I love roses planted with natives such as oioi, anemanthele, or muehlenbeckia.

Primula japonica ballantrae
BOG PRIMULA
This is a delightful marginal plant that grows best along the banks of a stream or small pond.

Clivia spp.
CLIVIA
Though clivia may require patience to grow en masse, once established it is the ideal groundcover beneath large trees.

Rudbeckia hirta
GLORIOSA DAISY
Another great perennial for large drifts of planting. Beautiful with gossamer grass, restiads and the foliage of *Coprosma* 'Red Rocks'.

Canna spp.
CANNA
Planted en masse or as highlights in a border, canna are drought-resistant and easy-care.

Lobelia cardinalis 'Queen Victoria'
LIBELIA 'QUEEN VICTORIA'
Great for around ponds. Varieties grown for the cut-flower market tend to have the best flower heads and a broader range of colours.

Chondropetalum tectorum
RESTIO
This hardy South African plant renews from the centre, making it a clean grower that stays looking its best throughout the year.

Phormium tenax
FLAX
This large flax often outgrows suburban gardens but in the country is ideal as a feature plant in large containers or used to fence paddocks.

Heliotropium arborescens
CHERRY PIE
This plant is a beautiful and fragrant companion to *Corokia* 'Grey Ghost' and *Astelia* 'Silver Spear'.

Salvia spp.
SALVIA
One of the hardiest of perennials and very free-flowering through most seasons. The colours are wonderful. Plant with native divaricating shrubs and grasses.

Gladiolus spp.
GLADIOLI
Must be one of the most cheerful of bulbs, appearing in colours that are simply iridescent. Easy to grow and great for mass plantings.

Hyacinthus spp.
HYACINTH
Plant close to living areas or paths to make the most of this fragrance. The flowers are beautifully formed and come in purples, pinks and whites.

Narcissus spp.
DAFFODIL
Whether lining a driveway or sweeping beneath a grove of trees, daffodils work best en masse. Plant in the hundreds if you can!

OTHER PLANTS TO CONSIDER

TREES

Juglans regia
WALNUT

Robinia spp.
MOP TOP, BLACK LOCUST

SHRUBS AND SMALL TREES

Viburnum spp.
SNOWBALL BUSH

Pyracantha coccinea
FIRETHORN

Syringa vulgaris
LILACS

Berberis thunbergii
JAPANESE BARBERRY

HARDY PERENNIALS

Kniphofia spp.
RED HOT POKER

Crocosmia spp.
CROCOSMIA
Closely related to gladioli. Wonderful planted in large sweeping drifts and can be mixed through a fresh green grass such as *Lomandra* spp.

Narcissus jonquilla
JONQUIL
Part of the daffodil family, the jonquil is one of the sweetest scented bulbs. Ideal planted close to paths.

THE NATURAL
Beekeeper's
Garden

When I was young, there were two hives in our garden in the Auckland suburbs. Our house and the garden were fairly well-populated: we had budgies, canaries, an axolotl, a tortoise, doves, quail, guppies, goldfish, finches, mice and cats. (The most recent resident is a lonely duck, who follows my mother with desperate loyalty.) When my mother decided to get hives it didn't seem especially out of the ordinary to us. Many of my friends did not agree, and were terrified of our wild backyard.

▲ **PREVIOUS PAGES** Beehives, even in their most standard form, can be cheerfully painted to bring character to a garden.

Easy-to-grow bog sage is one of the honey bee's favourites and is ideal for boggy clay soils.

WE ALL ENJOYED the ritual of my mother climbing into her spacesuit, grabbing her smoking gun and lifting open the humming box to bring out the rich honeycomb. We certainly suffered more stings than the average family and in more extraordinary places. I remember my mother looking quite terrifying with a fat lip, and I was slightly disheartened to have a swollen eye two weeks before I took the starring role as a princess in the school play. But despite the suffering we were all fond of these humming creatures and their collective efforts were a treat for all.

When I first started gardening, trimming a lavender hedge in full flower was a dangerous task. There was even a recommendation in our health and safety guide that those with allergies avoid this task. Now the lavender hedge in my front garden rarely has a single honey bee on it; the bumble bees are plentiful but the absence of the sweet honey bee is very obvious.

When exactly this change occurred I'm not sure, but it's fifteen years since I started my gardening business and it's quite pronounced. However, I have noticed that in neighbourhoods where there are good numbers of urban and suburban beekeepers you will see the bees. With or without bees of your own, you can help support efforts to retain healthy bee populations by planting a garden bees will enjoy. Creating suburban environments that are bee havens, and bee corridors that are free from chemicals, can be achieved one backyard at a time.

To manage a hive yourself you need to ensure that your property is suited and to be certain that you are prepared to commit to the management of the hive. If you have a great site but are not looking to become a beekeeper, there are plenty of keen beekeepers around who are happy to come to an agreement where they place their hives in your garden and you share costs and returns. The advantage to this is not just plenty of local honey; if you have fruit trees and other crops that are likely to be pollinated by bees (which is most fruiting edibles), you are likely to see a substantial increase in yield.

You should also assess what sort of food sources are available as bees need a constant supply of flowering plants. If there are stands of manuka close by — perhaps in a local park or stand of bush — or if you live next to a grove of pohutukawa, you can count them as part of the flowering stock your bees are likely to thrive on.

Ideally bees like plants en masse. You will notice that the flavour of your honey changes with the seasons as they feed on different flowers. You also need to think about the bees' flight path, which must be sheltered, ideally with morning sun. They need a clear runway in front of the hive, so think about where it's pointing; lining your flight path up with the neighbours' front entrance or their outdoor dining area may cause the sort of friction that even gifts of jars of honey won't resolve. Bees also enjoy supping from swimming pools, so this is worth taking into account, especially if the owner of the pool has allergies.

Keep the hive or hives clear of high-traffic areas and also the clothesline. Bees, like all creatures, are inclined to relieve themselves just before they make it home and if the washing is in the path it will end up stained with bee poop.

If you decide to take on a hive it's essential that you align yourself and keep in constant contact with a local association of beekeepers. There are several pests and diseases, including the destructive American foulbrood and the varroa mite, that devastate bee populations and it is important you are vigilant at identification so that if there is an outbreak you can prevent it spreading to other hives.

It is important to monitor your hives and keep them clear of wasps, which can decimate a single hive in a matter of weeks.

Design guide

CONSTANT FLOWERING

BEES ARE EASY to feed in the height of summer, when our gardens are full of blooms, but they need a supply of pollen in nectar throughout

◄ LEFT Echium is a great example of the iridescent blues that so appeal to bees. Three or four clumps will be enough to keep a hive happy during flowering.

the year, especially if you are going to steal their winter reserves of honey. If they have to, bees can travel up to eleven kilometres from the hive to gather honey, but if they have to travel much further than six kilometres, the energy it takes is not worth the honey made. So while you can depend on a greater food-gathering area than just your own backyard, you need to do an inventory of the plant material within a six-kilometre radius and to keep an eye on it so you can be assured that your bees are likely to be getting what they need. A garden on a cliff top or right next to a major motorway is not as good for bees as one that is plumb in the middle of a leafy suburb.

If you are depending on the surrounding areas to feed your bees, you also need to be aware of the likelihood of pesticide use. If your rural property, for example, is close to market gardens or orchards it is likely there will be large-scale chemical usage. Similarly if you live in city suburbs where a lot of your neighbours employ gardeners, it is also likely that there is relatively heavy use of sprays; in my experience people are always more comfortable getting someone else to apply chemicals than using them themselves. Pesticides are considered one of the major contributors to the decline in the bee population, along with other stresses of commercial honey production, so if you are making the commitment to keep bees then you need to accept that you'll be keeping the pesticides at bay.

You could consider sharing the cost and running of hives with a group of neighbours so that you can spread blocks of planting and the benefits of bees through your different gardens.

BLUES

FROM LAVENDER AND ECHIUM to salvias or catmint, the colour blue is a honey bee's favourite. They can spot a blue flower from afar, and upon it they will roll euphoric in the pollen. The more electric the blue, the more speedily they will find it, and once one bee discovers a patch of blue they return to the hive and do a complex dance that shows the other bees where to go and tells them what plant it is. Before you know it you'll have the whole hive on one patch. This is why bees like blocks of planting; if there is a block that the whole hive can feed from it is most efficient.

SPECIES

BEES PREFER SPECIES to cultivars. Species are the original variety of a plant rather than a selected cultivar or hybrid. They also prefer an open single blossom rather than the complicated double-petalled beauties that are popular with plant breeders. There is an increasing interest in species in the world of horticulture. After years of plant breeding, many breeders are even returning to the original varieties in the wild and looking for new characteristics. Conservationists, too, are focused on species and the natural variation within.

NATIVES

WE TEND TO ASSOCIATE BEES with the flowers of introduced plant varieties and it's easy to overlook how many flowers our native trees can hold in one bloom. There's manuka, of course, and the cabbage tree (which is actually the world's largest lily), which both have wonderful blooms for bees. Even our native flax is visited by honey bees.

There are, however, a couple of natives that are not at all bee-friendly. When tutu, or *Coriaria* spp., is fed on by vine hoppers, it produces a honeydew that will make the honey the bees eventually make very toxic to humans. The poisoning can be fatal. And as for the bees themselves, karaka gets them decidedly drunk, followed by bouts of disorientation and diarrhoea.

TREES AND SHRUBS

Metrosideros excelsa
POHUTUKAWA
Our beloved Christmas tree also makes some of the finest honey. Natives play just as important a role in honey production as exotic flowers.

Cordyline australis
CABBAGE TREE
Not actually a tree but a very, very tall perennial lily. Spring flowers buzz with bees.

Leptospermum scoparium
MANUKA
Manuka honey's medicinal properties are well known. However, to get a pure honey you need to gather it in careful timing with a large local flowering.

Prunus spp.
CHERRY TREE
Bees like cherries and other pip fruit, both ornamental and fruiting. Avoid double-petal varieties.

Citrus spp.
CITRUS
The fragrant flowers of citrus are often overlooked by inexperienced gardeners but never by bees.

PERENNIALS

Salvia uliginosa
BOG SAGE
Wonderful on the outskirts of a vegetable garden or around an orchard. Keep it out of main beds as it will quickly take over.

Thymus vulgaris
THYME
Plant en masse up a path or around a garden edge to keep bees happy for long periods.

Salvia leucantha
MEXICAN BUSH SAGE
Growing to around one metre tall, this loves the heat and resents overwatering. Perfect for a harsher coastal environment.

Cynara cardunculus var. *scolymus*
GLOBE ARTICHOKE
Rated for its stunning silver thistle-like leaves, breathtaking flowers and, if picked before flowering, its delicious buds. Will perform in dry clay soils.

Rosmarinus prostratus
ROSEMARY
This aromatic herb is so versatile from full sun to dappled shade. As long as the soil is free draining you should have little trouble.

Lavandula spp.
LAVENDER
Another great plant for bees. A lavender hedge is an effective way to provide bees with an ample and long-lasting supply of pollen.

Penstemon spp.
PENSTEMON
You will notice small stripes on the petals of these flowers, which are the equivalent of landing strips for bees and other insects.

Eryngium spp.
SEA HOLLY
These spiky-looking flowers may be designed to discourage grazing but their electric-blue hue shimmers like gold to bees.

Salvia farinacea
SALVIA
Another great salvia and readily available. Can be grown as an annual or as a perennial if pruned back at the end of autumn.

Rubus idaeus
RASPBERRY
Not only are these a sweet treat for the summer holiday, they are also loved by bees. The garden is kind to the beekeeper.

Nepeta x *faassenii*
CATMINT
This heat-loving, easy-care plant flowers for long periods and is great as a garden border, providing a good consistent supply for bees.

Echinacea spp.
ECHINACEA
This all-rounder goes to sleep at night with the hum of both bumble and honey bees.

Rosa spp.
ROSE
Single-petalled varieties are most appealing to honey bees. If you can source species roses these are ideal.

Passiflora spp.
PASSIONFRUIT

The relationship between the passionfruit flower and bees is symbiotic: sweet nectar in return for pollination.

Scabiosa spp.
SCABIOSA

This fluffy flower can be grown en masse in a range of circumstances. It also appeals to butterflies.

Phormium tenax
FLAX

May not look flowery or even have the blue colour that bees are so attracted to, but bees love it as much as birds do.

Achillea spp.
ACHILLEA

Easy to grow through an orchard with comfrey and other woodland herbs. Will support bees, which are needed to pollinate fruit.

ANNUALS

Delphinium spp.
DELPHINIUM

Good for maintaining a pollen source through summer months. It's in this plant's interests to attract bees, since it is dependant on them for pollination.

Borago officinalis
BORAGE

Great to sow around orchards and boundaries near vegetable gardens. Flowers can be used in ice cubes for summer drinks.

Nigella spp.
LOVE IN A MIST

Can be grown from seed or often available in punnets. It's easy to see why the bees are attracted to these delightful flowers.

Helianthus annuus
SUNFLOWER

Great planted up a narrow drive, these giants don't need a large garden to grow as long as they can head for the sky.

Brassica spp.
BRASSICA

This is a large family which includes cabbages, broccoli and cauliflowers. If left to seed after the main harvests, the flowers are very desirable for bees.

OTHER PLANTS TO CONSIDER

TREES AND SHRUBS

Metrosideros carminea
RATA

Prunus dulcis
ALMONDS

Knightia excelsa
REWAREWA

Callistemon spp.
BOTTLEBRUSH

Pittosporum tenuifolium
LEMONWOOD

PERENNIALS

Centaurea montana
CORNFLOWER

Perovskia spp.
RUSSIAN SAGE

Verbena spp.
VERBENA

Convolvulus mauritanicus
GROUND MORNING GLORY

Veronica spp.
VERONICA

THE NATURAL
Native
Garden

With over two-and-a-half thousand species native to our shores and many of them unique, the native New Zealand garden is rich and varied. It is easy to take the textures and muted tones of our plants for granted, but see them through a visitor's eyes and they are undoubtedly exotic. Also to be celebrated are the regional variations that can be found across the country.

▲ **PREVIOUS PAGE** *Apodasmia similis*, the native reed commonly known as oioi, is tolerant of both wet and dry conditions and of poor soils. It's a wonderful plant for textural plantings.

▶ **RIGHT** *Chionochloa flavicans* or miniature toetoe, planted here alongside muehlenbeckia, is one of my favourite plants. When I once used it in a garden at the Chelsea Flower Show we were charged £75 per plant as a hire fee!

FOR A LANDSCAPE designer this palette of plants is all the more exciting as we have the opportunity to discover and use new plants in ways they have never been used before. *Selliera radicans*, for example, is a coastal herb which makes an extraordinarily hardy lawn alternative. As well as having a beautiful fresh green colour, its coastal origins mean it can be dosed with sea water to eliminate other weeds. Never needing trimming, and flowering with white star-like flowers through summer, it is a perfect lawn alternative for the suburban garden.

Here's another example. The kowhai tree has long been popular, but not so many gardeners are familiar with the prostrate kowhai *Sophora prostrata*, which grows no taller than two metres (it is slow growing so don't hold your breath) with beautiful twisting stems that weep downwards. This compact plant is an excellent feature plant for smaller gardens, having an almost oriental feel that's similar to a dwarf weeping Japanese maple.

Treasures like these are continually being discovered among our native flora and they are what make having a native garden such a journey of discovery. Long gone are the days where a native garden was a simple planting of a row of flax and a few cabbage trees. These days a growing awareness of, and access to, the diversity of native plant material can not only ignite our interest but also helps preserve our national treasures.

Te Kainga Marire, a small suburban garden in the heart of New Plymouth designed by Valda Poletti and David Clarkson, is a stellar example of how wonderfully rich and complex a slice of suburbia can be. Inspired by a love of both plants and the mountains, the garden is a journey from a moss-laden path lined with ferns, through an underground tunnel of ferns and delicate native orchids, out through a bush garden, through a kitchen garden and out onto an alpine plateau. Enter another path, and you discover a wetland. Hidden down the drive is a slowly running waterfall.

While this sounds like a lot to fit on one section, it works effectively because the plants have been carefully selected for their suitability to the different aspects of the site. The site isn't flat, and its curving

form creates a range of different environments. After all, gardens are never single entities; what blooms on one side of a house is most likely to struggle on the other. This is an opportunity to have a range of garden environments in which to experiment and play. This sort of ecologically styled planting is a wonderful way to set the theme for your native garden. A south-facing site with volcanic soil and high rainfall will allow you to grow a range of ferns and groundcovers that would struggle on a hot garden site, while an exposed rockery is a great opportunity to look at our alpine plants and perhaps even coastal varieties.

Plants that are meant to grow together have a harmony to them, a natural style of their own that makes sense to our eyes.

It also looks good. Plants that are meant to grow together have a harmony to them, a natural style of their own that makes sense to our eyes. Rules are made to be broken, of course, but there are some key elements that will guide you. In general, a plant that's suited to a hot arid site signals that preference via its leaves and form: the silvery blue foliage of *Festuca coxii* or the orange hues of *Libertia peregrinans* are a good example. Put these colours in with soft green ferns and they look out of place, perhaps even garish, but locate them in a stony cliff-top garden with *Pachystegia* spp. and *Celmisia* spp., both alpine plants with silver-toned foliage, and the effect is brilliant.

ONCE YOU'VE DECIDED the 'ecology' of the different zones of your site, the joyful challenge is to discover what plants are best suited to them. The best field trip is a trip into the wild, to see our native plants as they've chosen to grow. The best nurserymen do their research here, as origin is the key to a plant's secrets. A plant that grows in the cracks of rocks does so for the warmth and moisture that is reflected from the stone and held in its seam. Looking at plants in the wild can also help you understand conundrums such as why nikau will sometimes, but

not always, grow well in full sun. Shelter is normally desirable to start, but as the palm finds the sun it is more than happy to bask in it.

Specialty nurseries are the best place to go when seeking plants for a native garden as they are more likely to be staffed by experts who have more than an inkling about what natives need to grow. They are also the guardians of a broader and more complex range of plant material suited to a wide range of growing conditions; whatever your situation they can guide you to something really special.

Geoff Davidson of the Oratia Native Plant Nursery, near Auckland, is such a man. He's spent his life studying how best to propagate native plant material for garden and landscape settings. To him we owe the popularity of natives such as the lush and leafy native climber *Tecomanthe speciosa*, which at one point was on the brink of extinction. He has also discovered a unique variety of what was originally thought to be a native *Veronica* spp. but has now been renamed *Parahebe jovellanoides*. This small but free-flowering perennial is now available to gardeners despite there only being one known small colony in the wild.

There is something deeply satisfying about knowing that the plants in your garden are select and unique. Some gardeners find being responsible for a plant whose numbers are so few a great weight to bear but the truth is quite the opposite. It is through the trials and errors of gardeners that we've learnt more about these plants; even our failures can unlock another piece of the jigsaw to ensure they are preserved for future generations.

▶ RIGHT This shot demonstrates the distinctive textures of our native divaricates. Here, *Coprosma* 'Red Rocks', *Muehlenbeckia astoni* and *Coprosma* 'Dark Spire' merge to create a moody coastal theme.

Design guide

TAMING TEXTURE

THE CHARACTERISTIC THAT most defines our native plants, and separates them from exotics, is texture. The range of leaf types in our various environments is vast, running from the tiny seed-like leaves of divaricates and the graphic forms of *Pseudopanax* spp. to large leafy trees such as *Meryta sinclairii* (puka) or *Griselinia littoralis* (kapuka). Grasses and reeds, too, add another element of fine lineal form in a broad range of colour. When layered upon each other, or even used in sweeping blocks, these plants sing, and gardeners can use them as if they were creating a tapestry. Generally I've found that unless there's a backdrop such as a building or an ocean outlook to be silhouetted against, fine-leaved divaricating plants such as muehlenbeckia and corokia and fine-leafed trees such as ribbonwood should be brought forward in a composition. If they are pushed back behind bolder leaves they can be lost.

Think, too, about what light does to texture. One of my favourite plants, *Anemanthele lessoniana*, changes colour as the different lights hit it, an effect that is especially apparent when it's carrying its autumnal tones. The slight shimmer to its fine leaves throws the light around, especially in the morning and at dusk. It grows naturally on the bush border, making it an excellent garden plant, given that a garden border with trees and shrubs behind and open plantings in front mimics the planting arrangements of its wild habitat.

Strong forms such as nikau or Chatham Island forget-me-nots can be given space by underplantings of native groundcover. Those I've had most success with in the landscape are the many *Leptinella* spp. as well as *Muehlenbeckia axillaris*, which is incredibly hardy and grows in a wide range of conditions. *Pimelea prostrata* is very hardy for full sun and offers a nice alternative in colour with its silver-blue foliage and star-white flowers.

◀ **LEFT** What I love most about this planting at Te Kainga Marire is the way the prostrate kowhai subjugates its twisting form to the dominating ponga. The bird bath sits within this tangled scene like an offering to the bird gods.

Our native plants also offer some great texture for hedging. Totara, both golden and blue, are excellent hedging plants with a wonderfully fine-pointed leaf. Coprosma can range from a glossy green to a deep, rich brown, and griselinia are a tried and true option with a fresh, green, larger leaf.

MORE THAN JUST PLANTS

ONE OF THE joys of a native garden is that you are not just preserving and gaining an understanding of our local plant material; with it comes a wonder of other creatures. Some, like the tui, we are very familiar with, and others ecologists and biologists are just beginning to understand. I once was discussing bugs with an entomologist, who told me that the mealy bug on my flax that so frustrated me was actually most likely a native that had as much right to be there as the flax. At the same time he happened to mention a small native slug that also lived on the flax. Weeks later, as I pulled the damaged leaves off at the base of a flax plant, I discovered this small, jewel-like insect. Never did I imagine I would call a slug a jewel yet this leaf-veined almost translucent creature shimmered like kauri gum. While the mealy bug is not encouraged in my garden, and swiftly pruned away (I'm sure it will survive without me), I am delighted to have found that even slugs (of the right breeding) can bring a moment of pleasure in a garden.

The main key to attracting birds and other critters to the garden is providing them with a rich and plentiful food supply. This is a plant lover's pleasure as it means packing your garden with treats that berry and flower the year through. While focusing on trees and shrubs that supply nectar and fruit will enrich your garden, remember that every plant has a role in an ecosystem; even those that don't carry food are likely to carry insects that offer birds a snack.

SCALE

THE MAIN MISTAKE new gardeners are likely to make when they plan a native garden is to underestimate the eventual scale of some native trees. This doesn't mean that trees shouldn't be planted but rather that you need to consider how their scale will impact on not just your own property but also the surrounding landscape. If you border a reserve, large trees may have a lot to offer both you and the community, creating a lovely transition between the two. If your garden slopes steeply downhill, you may be able to comfortably plant trees at the base of the slope where you can enjoy their canopy — but do give a thought to neighbours below, for whom your trees may eventually be a problem. Overplanting a garden can be a fine approach if it is properly managed and if you are prepared to thin out superfluous trees as the garden matures. Don't leave this too late, however: overplanting may ruin the shape of the trees you wish to keep long term, and depending on current tree laws there may be restrictions on the size of larger trees that can be removed.

Our natural flora includes forest giants, but there are plenty of smaller trees well suited to suburban gardens. Kowhai and kaka beak are compact trees, and varieties such as puka can be heavily pruned to maintain a good size. Nikau and cabbage trees have a slender form that allows height in a narrow space; planted in layers they can be very effective.

THE NARRATIVE

WHILE PERHAPS not part of the aesthetic of your garden, there is great pleasure in knowing its story. This is especially true of our native plants, which have histories both distant and immediate that are taonga in themselves. Some have medicinal uses, some have been returned from the brink of extinction, some have berries that are important to an endemic skink and some may have been propagated from seed by a dear friend who passed them to you. These 'back-stories' inform our

love of plants and engage others with our gardens. Knowing and telling such stories comes naturally to gardeners; this is how our knowledge of the natural world has been conveyed from one generation to the next. I've learnt so much from gardeners who have passed native-plant knowledge on to me.

FLOWERS

IT IS TRUE that our native flora lacks an abundance of flowery perennials such as the wild flowers of the Americas or the extravagant trumpets of colour found in the plants of the tropics. The tones of our natives are more muted, less showy; and rather than having distinctive individual blooms they present best en masse. Think of pohutukawa blanketed in red, or kowhai in bloom, then turn your mind to manuka and hebes, all carpeted in flowers for good lengths of time. Cabbage trees have splendid sweet-smelling blooms; there's an impressive architecture in *Xeronema callistemon*'s brush-like red stamens and its sword-like foliage; the native brooms carmichaelia offer pinks and yellows on their seaweed-like forms. The perception that our plants are relatively flowerless is because, in most regions of the country, they seldom lose their foliage and so the ratio of flowers to green appears reduced. Certainly in warmer areas of the country, with high rainfall, the foliage can be so abundant that we don't yearn quite so much for the flowers of spring given that we haven't suffered the discomfort of a truly cold winter. This would explain why the flower-garden tradition is so much stronger in cooler regions of the country. Plants in warmer areas do not need to produce in such a self-sacrificing manner as the perennials of changeable landscapes where a snowy winter may last four months of a year, or where wildfires may decimate the landscape, demanding constant renewal. But once you begin to notice not just the flowers but also the berries that are characteristic of so many of our plants, you'll be smitten. They can't compare with the 'show-pony' plants of other lands but there's much delight — both in colour and form — to be found in the creamy blooms of our native hibiscus or the yellow stars on a corokia's black stems.

◀ **LEFT** Having a natural garden does not mean that our living areas should lack simplicity and function. Here in one of my Auckland gardens (far left) simple concrete slabs are brought to life by tumbling plantings of my favourite native groundcovers *Selliera radicans* and, close to the volcanic boulders dug up from the site, *Muehlenbeckia axillaris*. The totara hedge makes a simple but effective screen.

In this recreation of my Chelsea project at Matamata (main image) I approached the planting as if it were a revegetation project. In this first stage I've planted hardy primary species that will create the environment for a second generation of plants to thrive.

MATERIAL

THE NATIVE GARDEN is often associated with a rustic style: railway-sleeper steps, kiwiana-styled corrugated iron fences, paua shells scattered around the bases of cleverly crafted stone towers is a well-known 'look'. Such gardens deserve to be celebrated, but the native garden offers plenty of other interpretations and iterations. Native gardens work beautifully with the strong clean lines of contemporary architecture, their austere simplicity helping link both house and owner to the environment. The original modernists never intended that gardens would be stripped back in a minimalist approach. Instead they saw nature and the richness of gardens as a wonderful contrast with a clean and well-organised living environment. Frank Lloyd Wright was a wonderful gardener and collector of plants, and his skilful plant combinations are echoed by such present-day landscape designers as Piet Oudolf.

The ability to capture in a garden the mood of nature, in all its changeable forms, is a triumph of mastery and magic, the work of a lifetime.

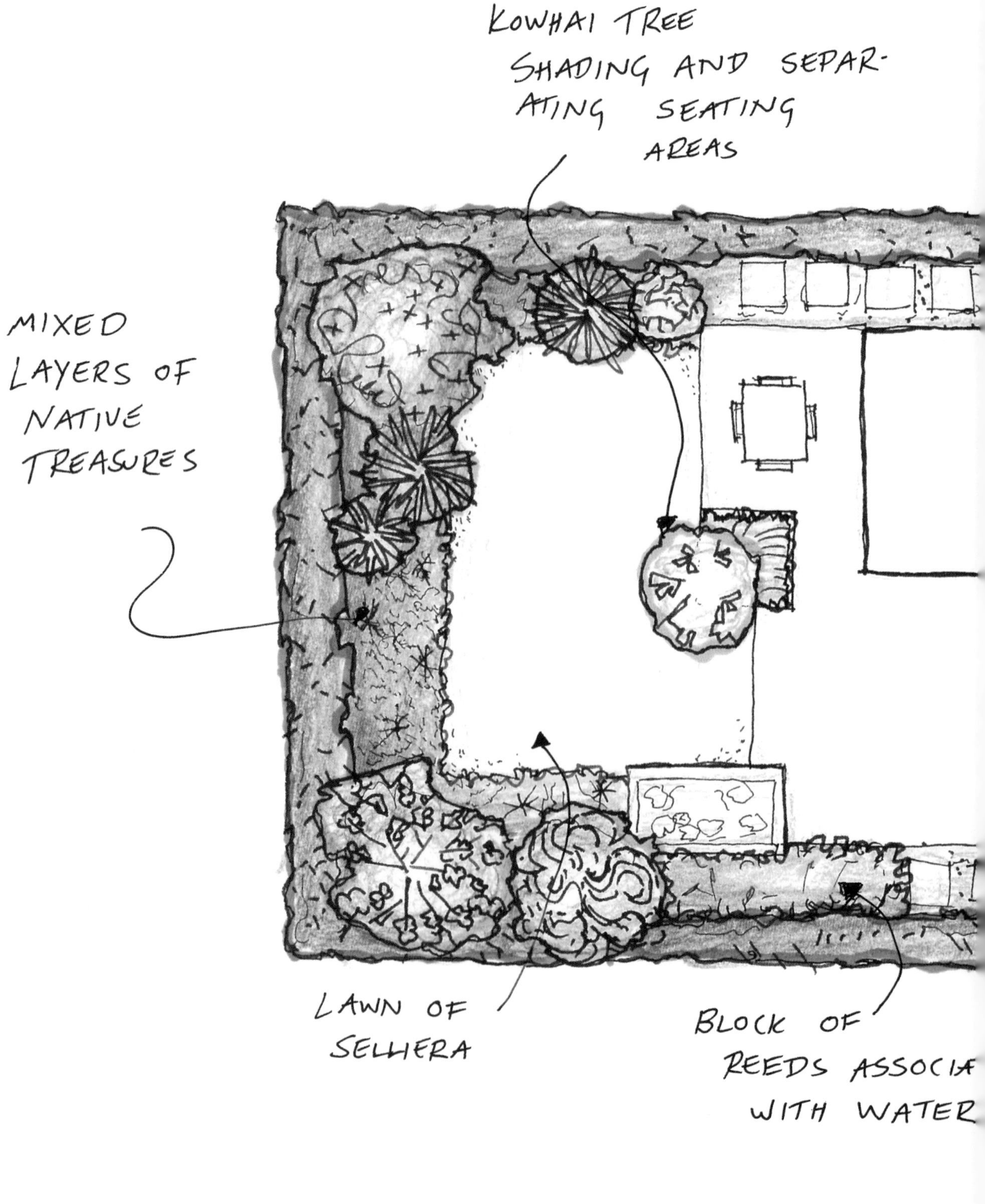

KOWHAI TREE
SHADING AND SEPAR-
ATING SEATING
AREAS

MIXED
LAYERS OF
NATIVE
TREASURES

LAWN OF
SELLIERA

BLOCK OF
REEDS ASSOCIA
WITH WATER

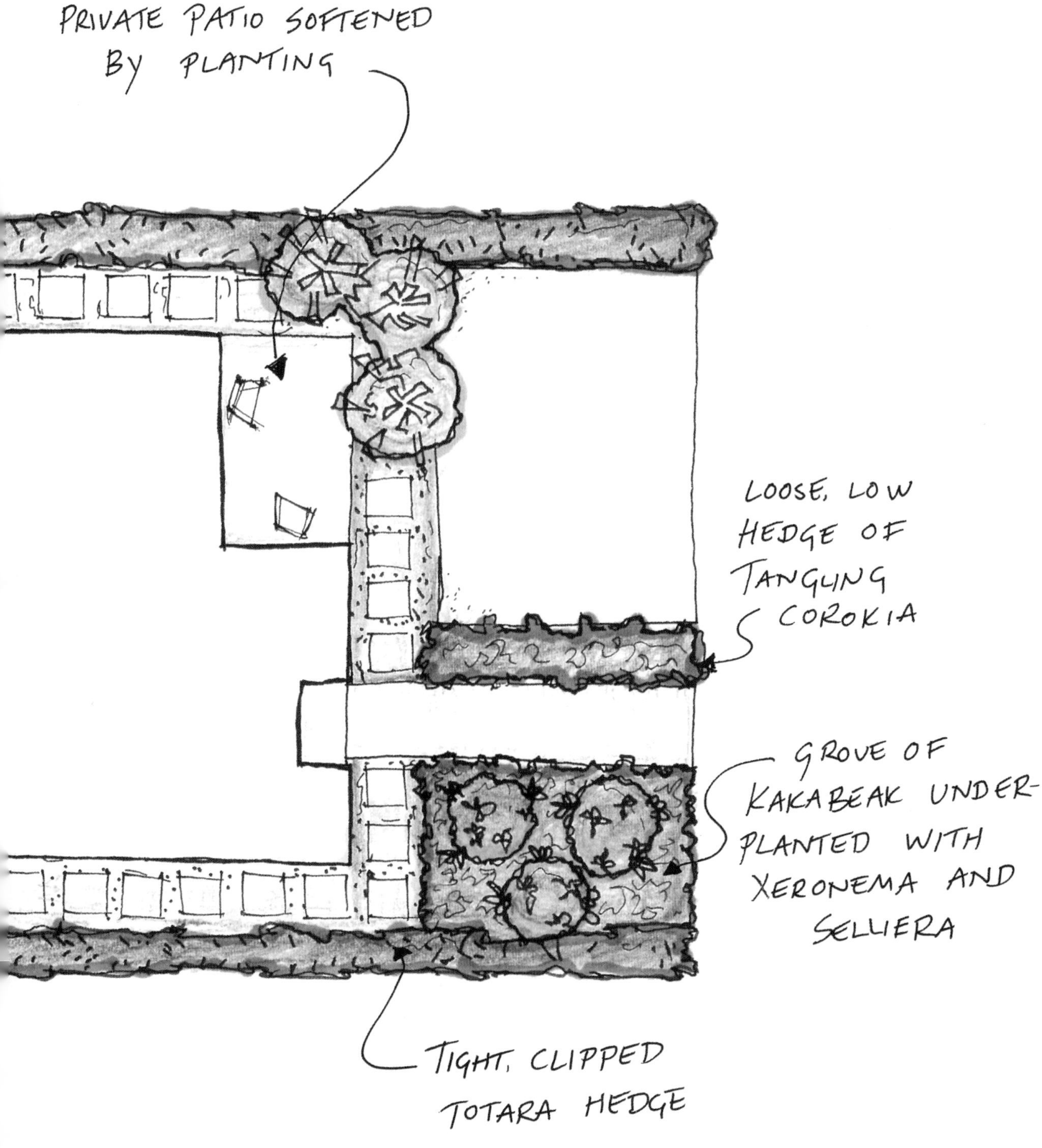

PRIVATE PATIO SOFTENED
BY PLANTING

LOOSE, LOW
HEDGE OF
TANGLING
COROKIA

GROVE OF
KAKABEAK UNDER-
PLANTED WITH
XERONEMA AND
SELLIERA

TIGHT, CLIPPED
TOTARA HEDGE

TREES

Carpodetus spp.
PUTAPUTAWETA
Doesn't look particularly spectacular in a nursery but once the light hits its marbled leaves its beauty is revealed. Grows well in heavy clay soils in a south-facing garden.

Sophora microphylla
KOWHAI
An attractive fine-leafed form of kowhai and the most common. Its size is ideal for most gardens. There are many varieties: choose one that is endemic to your area.

Cyathea medullaris
MAMAKU
This amazing tree fern will grow in full sun and has the most splendid black velvet trunk beneath huge fronds. A stand-out specimen.

Plagianthus regius
RIBBONWOOD
A wonderful small tree where delicate texture is desired. Its soft form and sparse leaves make it good for soft screening.

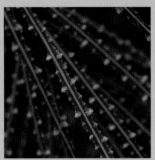

Pseudopanax ferox
TOOTHED LANCEWOOD
Has the most unusual juvenile form. As the tree matures, it takes on an attractive pompom shape. Suitable for sandy soils.

Clianthus spp.
KAKA BEAK
One of the showier natives. When in full bloom, its branches appear near breaking point with the weight of flowers. Prone to caterpillars but still well worth growing.

SHRUBS

Coprosma spp.
COPROSMA
From glossy green to bronze or even rainbow foliage, a hardy and attractive plant for hedging, groundcover, topiary and screening.

Corokia spp.
COROKIA
Wonderful texture in any garden. Also a wonderful plant for topiary and adds good structure to a garden for a patio or entrance.

Macropiper melchior
THREE KINGS KAWAKAWA
A wonderful plant. With heart-shaped shiny green leaves, *M. melchior* is more resilient to the insects that leave threads of holes through the leaves.

Brachyglottis repanda
PURPUREA

The foliage of this beautiful shrub has the most amazing contrast, with purple faces of the leaves and white undersides and stem.

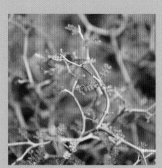

Sophora prostrata
DWARF KOWHAI

A must-have in a native garden. Its orange twisting form weeps and is covered in small round leaves. The small flowers are an orangey-yellow.

Clematis paniculata
CLEMATIS

A wonderful native climber for a fence or tree. Its roots must be kept cool. Will climb to full sun in a sheltered position.

Tecomanthe speciosa
THREE KINGS VINE

A dramatic and vigorous climber with lush green leaves and mildly fragrant cream flowers. Excellent for vertical green screens.

TEXTURE, PERENNIALS AND GROUNDCOVER

Anemanthele lessoniana
GOSSAMER GRASS

The drooping form with flowers is both graceful and tidy. The seed heads are an added pleasure in the spring garden.

Euphorbia glauca
NATIVE EUPHORBIA

This delightful euphorbia grows to just 300–400mm high, making it a good compact highlight in a smaller garden.

Elatostema rugosum
PARATANIWHA

Perfect for a shaded green wall with good irrigation, this New Zealand native has wonderful fresh green and bronze leaves.

Phormium cookianum
MOUNTAIN FLAX

While *P. tenax* is often too large for most gardens, *P. cookianum* is a great alternative, remaining compact and tidy. Equally loved by birds.

Gunnera prorepens
CREEPING GUNNERA

With stiff leather-like leaves, the highlight of this plant is the bright red fruit which develops in February and remains for several weeks.

Muehlenbeckia spp.
MUEHLENBECKIA
All three species are excellent: *M. astonii* is a great mounding shrub, *M. axillaris* a hardy groundcover and *M. complexa* to train up or down walls.

Geranium traversii var. *elegans*
CHATHAM ISLAND GERANIUM
One of our native geraniums, this shallow-rooting perennial has the compact growth appropriate for a shallow soil medium.

Hibiscus richardsonii and *Hibiscus diversifolius*
NATIVE HIBISCUS
Both have attractive seed heads and flowers. Though best treated as an annual, will happily self-sow.

Xeronema callistemon
POOR KNIGHTS LILY
Performs best in containers with a stony growing medium. Red plumes are formed in summer.

Pimelea prostrata
NEW ZEALAND DAPHNE
This sprawling groundcover is wonderful between rocks and very attractive when carpeted in its softly fragrant white flowers.

Dracophyllum sinclairii
NEINEI
This native grows free-standing in a sheltered garden. Slow-growing but with a beautiful slender form.

Chionochloa flavicans
MINI TOETOE
A wonderful landscape grass. Similar in appearance to a toetoe but smaller and softer-leafed, this is a more suitable option for the home garden.

Selliera radicans
REMUREMU
A hardy groundcover and wonderful lawn alternative, carpeted in white flowers in summer. Weeds can be controlled with occasional doses of sea water.

Carmichaelia australis
NATIVE BROOM
This native broom is a splendid garden plant that is endangered in many of its natural habitats.

FERNS

Blechnum procerum
SMALL KIOKIO
This stiff-leafed fern adds great texture and makes an excellent garden plant. Beautiful planted in sweeps beneath nikau or mamaku.

Blechnum montanum
MOUNTAIN FERN
Has a beautiful, crisp form and is tolerant of cooler climates. Like most blechnum, it has an attractive red flush to new growth.

Asplenium bulbiferum
HEN AND CHICKEN FERN
This dependable garden plant spores young plants over its mature fronds. These are easily transplanted for propagation.

OTHER PLANTS TO CONSIDER

TREES

Elingamita johnsonii
ELINGAMITA

Aristotelia serrata
WINEBERRY

Rhopalostylis sapida
NIKAU

SHRUBS

Pseudowintera colorata
MOUNTAIN HOROPITO

Dodonaea viscosa
AKEAKE

Ackama rosaefolia
MAKAMAKA

TEXTURES, PERENNIALS AND GROUNDCOVER

Pachystegia spp.
MARLBOROUGH ROCK DAISY

Parahebe spp.
SNOW CAP

Isotoma spp.
BLUE STAR CREEPER

Fuchsia procumbens
CREEPING FUCHSIA

Libertia spp.
MIKOIKOI

CLIMBERS

Metrosideros carminea
RATA

Parsonsia capsularis var. *grandiflora*
AKAKIORE

FERNS

Doodia media
PUKUPUKU, RASP FERN

Adiantum hispidulum
ROSY MAIDENHAIR FERN

Pellaea rotundifolia
BUTTON FERN

Cyathea dealbata
SILVER FERN

THE NATURAL
Small
Garden

When we have land to spare, putting some aside for a garden is a no-brainer but for urban dwellers with increasingly shrinking sections and often large amounts of time spent away from a property, the whole notion of having and maintaining a garden can seem like a distant romance, something that you could do in a less harried era.

BUT IT NEED NOT BE. True, smaller spaces need to be treated with a greater level of efficiency but with good organisation you can, in fact, cram a decent amount into a small envelope of space. Lovingly nurtured pot plants are indeed enough to make a garden. It is, however, critical that you plan the garden with function in mind.

This should start with an honest appraisal of how you are best going to use the space. Your priorities could be growing food, cut flowers, bird song, a haven to withdraw from the world, or a place for children to play while adults entertain. It is then that the jigsaw puzzle begins.

Organising a space effectively is simply about finding the best arrangement of spaces to suit your lifestyle. Primary living spaces such as an entertaining area should always be given priority. Secondary living spaces or destinations, such as a spa pool or a kitchen garden, should be located for ease of use but do not necessarily need to have pride of space as they have an appeal that draws you to them.

Once you have rearranged the spaces according to their uses you will also be able to establish the flow of your garden, establishing where the high and low traffic areas will be. A front path is always treated as high traffic and should be a hard durable surface, while paths around a vegetable garden are probably fine in a permeable surface such as gravel.

It is also important to assess the site for prevailing winds and sun; a vegetable garden needs good sun, for example, while a spa pool will need shelter and intimacy. It is important to map out all these functions before you start thinking of the plants themselves, although of course existing plants need to come into the process early on. It's a good idea to take an inventory of the plants you have on-site, evaluating what's

◀ **LEFT** Much of the money we spend on expensive walling and garden structures can be more beautifully achieved, at a lower cost, with hedges and trees. Save it for focal points like this gate into the Dalton's Plantation courtyard, where the walls have been created with a hedge of Fairy Magnolia Blush, a cross between *Doltsopa* x *yunnanensis* x *figo*. The arch has been created by tying together the young tips of cherry trees. In spring it is a romantic entry, all for the cost of six young trees.

wrongly placed and needs transplanting or removing.

Once you have established the functionality of your space you can then consider what other practical functions planting could offer that will save you money that would otherwise be spent on hard landscaping and also help green up your outlook. Planting can screen unpleasant views, and create shelter from wind and shade from sun. It can also create a point of focus or frame an artwork. Plants are not only the 'furnishings' of our outdoor spaces, they also, with careful planning, form a significant part of the structure. Before you choose the plants that will adorn your garden, you should decide on the form of their 'bones'. How high should a hedge be, and could it step to open to more appealing views and rise to mask a neighbour's old shed? How large should a tree be to give you shade without robbing you of wanted sun? Do you need its form to be broad and wide or tall and lean? By making decisions such as these before you select the plant material you are more able to choose plants that will be well suited to your needs. All these decisions are likely to be the same whatever style of planting appeals to you the most.

> Plants are not only the 'furnishings' of our outdoor spaces, they also, with careful planning, form a significant part of the structure.

With the framework decided and the spaces clearly defined, it is then time for dressing up, exploring materials, and making choices based both on budget and the look of a space. Whether it's defined with decking or concrete or stone, a space will still function well. If a tall slender tree is required, a Bangalow palm may suit a tropical garden, a pawpaw or banana a productive garden, and a Japanese maple a flower garden. The native gardener may choose a cabbage tree or nikau. All these trees serve the same function. Take hedges. The subtropical garden will look great with a griselinia hedge, a productive garden could have feijoas, the flower garden a sweet-scented michelia, the native garden olearia or coprosma... these plants will all create a hedge of a similar height and form.

◄ **LEFT** Combining foliage and flowers offers the best of both worlds and gives a small space year-round interest as different flowers come in and out of season. Here Ralf Krüger combines *Ligularia przewalskii, Iris chrysographes* 'Black Form', *Euphorbia polychroma, Carex testacea* and *Hemerocallis citrina*.

WHILE FUNCTION SHOULD lead form, it is worth considering what depth can offer in a garden. It is a common mistake to push our living spaces close to the boundaries in order to make the most of our land, but does a deck or patio need to be large to be both functional and pleasant? In fact the opposite can often be the case. It is worth considering having a primary space such as a deck with large flowing steps that double as seating, leading to a secondary area when occasions require. As long as the spaces connect comfortably they can work better than one large open area. Make sure you consider your garden furniture, too, and how this will fit in to the overall planning of the garden.

With well-laid-out and functional living spaces you can afford to fill the gaps with layers of planting to provide year-round effect and seasonal pleasure. With the bones decided you can fill the gaps as you please but make sure you give the garden a rhythm and a theme, be it colour, texture or a style of plants. In even the loosest of plantings you need repetition and form, places for the eye to rest. These can be clipped shrubs, rocks, pots or an architecturally formed plant; whatever your choice, they will help to hold a composition and maintain order. The best thing about a well-laid-out structure is that it allows the rest of the garden to grow and soften, so it looks great even when you've been otherwise occupied and you can climb back into it, wanting nothing more than a day of pleasure in the garden — and not because you are burdened with guilt.

Repetition, it should be remembered, is how nature itself plays. Much like us, plants appear mainly in colonies and sub-colonies, with the odd loner taking pride of place here or there. Nature is never likely to dabble in one of this and one of that; before long there is a war of borders, with the dominant species fighting it out for pride of place in sun or shade. Nature demands order as much as we do, and it is the gardener's job to see that space is given to the various competitors so we can see the very best of their form.

Design guide

CONTAINERS

THE CONTAINER GARDEN is great for the gardener in transit. For more and more people, owning property is not the be all and end all, but this does not count you out as a gardener. For years I lived in a city-fringe apartment with a small balcony as the only outdoor space. This did not stop me adopting the many plant orphans that come my way in my line of work, both for inside and out.

In many ways container gardening is one of the most fun ways to get started. Your garden can be as big or as small as you wish and you can downgrade any time you want by showering friends and colleagues with green gifts. What you grow plants in is really up to you. I've seen gardens growing out of old guitars, suitcases and plumbing pipes. Containers can be hung, strung and balanced on or from almost anything. Keep in mind, though, that containers need drainage so you need a hole at the base for water to go. Ideally, too, you need a saucer, especially if pots are to sit on wooden decking that will quickly rot if pots are placed directly on top. If your flooring is timber, it pays to move the pots out and about every month or so to clean underneath. It helps the plants also if you rotate them, so the back side gets some light, preventing them developing a lopsided view on life.

As for what you can grow in containers, pretty much anything goes when it comes to creating a look. Strong form, edible, flowers, natives… all have options for containers. You can either fall in love with individual plants and find a pot to suit them or decide the form and colour you want and seek the plant.

FOCUS

IN A SMALLER GARDEN you need to consider your line of focus; more often than not you will be looking inwards rather than out beyond your garden. Identify the most important areas of focus by lining up views from significant windows and doors or seating areas. These are the points around which you draw your composition, too. You can place framing trees either side, place seating, or add water features or art. It can even be as simple as a pot. Be careful not to get carried away, and limit yourself to one or two hard features, doing the rest with planting. It can be as simple as framing a view to the garden with the arching branch of a tree.

WALLS AND FENCES

A WALL IS what I call a high-value landscape item. Whatever the material, a wall requires good foundations and must be well built. Walls, therefore, should be used to good effect, and not simply run all the way around a section unless expense is not a consideration. My view is that if you won't see it, then generally a fence painted black is just as effective for securing and defining a property as a fancy wall. In fact property boundaries are best not seen at all, and a garden that can borrow the best aspects of its surroundings while masking the hard edge of a fence is doing well. There is nothing wrong with 'borrowing' a neighbour's tree or even the top of a beautiful wall if it adds to your own garden's effect.

A wall should be considered an important design detail, one used for effect and to clearly define a space or provide a backdrop upon which to play. It may be that a section of a beautifully built wall is enough, with hedges either side hiding an ordinary fence. Never be afraid of a folly that lets you stretch your budget further than expected. Generally the further a boundary is from a house, the less likely it needs to be substantially defined. If you and your neighbours have closely aligned living areas, you may want a more solid divider, not just to provide privacy but also to soften sound.

IRRIGATION

WHETHER OR NOT you choose to put in an irrigation system depends as much on your own daily routines as it does on your climate and the scale of your garden. If your garden consists only of containers then watering, even daily, may be as much a part of the pleasure as the pottering in the garden itself. But containers need more regular watering than a garden, especially if they are in a covered outdoor area, and so if you are away for extended periods you do not want to end up losing your precious plants.

The rainfall of your region will also have a bearing on your decision. The shorter the dry periods, the less value you get from a watering system. However irrigation can be the most effective way of getting water directly to the roots of the plants, so reducing waste. If you are looking for a simple and flexible option rather than a professional system you can try a soaker hose on a timer. These are very effective at achieving good soil saturation with little waste.

LIGHTING

IN AN URBAN GARDEN the value of garden lighting is substantial. Having lighting can not only double the time you can spend in a garden space, it can also be used to create a magical outlook, whatever the weather. Even if it doesn't make the first budget round, ensure that you don't restrict yourself by not installing the electrics you'll need should you decide to add lights in the future. At the very least you could lay a conduit beneath any newly placed hard surfaces; this is as simple as placing a plastic tube that's adequate to thread wires through, through the substrate of a concrete pad before it is poured or beneath paving before it is laid. Ideally make a note of this on your house plans so that future owners know it's there if required.

My approach to lighting is to use small subtle spots to highlight the form and bones of a garden. Be careful not to create black holes in the middle of a space and make sure the light leads you through the areas you wish to be in. If you set up the spots on short wire runs, you can adjust them in the dark and as the garden grows. Never cut the wire so short that you have no leeway; the art is in the detail, and fine-tuning makes a world of difference to the overall effect.

Lighting should also be practical, with care given to illuminating such elements as steps that could be dangerous if unseen. Lit well, the clean horizontal lines of steps can be made a feature themselves.

Think, too, of the direction of lights and ensure you avoid shining them directly into eyes. A garden, unlike a house, is invariably on multiple levels and a light lined up in one area has the potential to cause a problem in another space, so make sure you assess the direction of light from the various areas. If you have a water feature, direct downward light can be used to create beautiful reflections on the water surface. This is not possible in all situations, however, and the right angle is required for it to work. I encourage people to experiment with a flashlight for special features such as this in order to avoid costly disappointments later.

Big trees need a bit of grunt when it comes to lighting, and unfortunately the size of light required is hard to mask during the day. It's best if you can place these larger spots between roots, or plant around them without obscuring them, as ideally we want to be surprised when the garden light is cast after dusk.

ESPALIER, WIRES AND FRAMES

A GOOD DEAL of getting the most out of a space comes from making use of more than one plane of living space. Even where space is limited, there is no reason not to enjoy a green outlook. It is now well

established that a green outlook is the best thing for reducing stress. Most of us know how quickly the bothers of the day lift away when we step outside into a beautifully designed space that is fresh and green. Even the most narrow garden rooms can be greened by the use of wire screens upon which climbers can be grown or by the art of espalier, which is training trees to grow flatly against a wall.

Not only is this an efficient way of greening a narrow space, it is also very effective and in fact was first developed to grow fruit trees such as pears and apples. For fruit production, ideally the wall should face the sun to assist ripening. Start with a young tree and as it grows, pull the still soft and flexible branches down so they are evenly spread or splayed against a wall. A wide range of shapes and forms is available, depending on the tree; take some time to plan the look you most prefer. This can also be done freestanding, with the branches trained to wires so they in time create a living fence. Make sure you use wires that are stainless steel. Unlike trees that will develop their own strength, climbers are more dependent on the strength of their growing frame and will collapse if it does.

THE SMALL TREE

THERE IS A LOT to be said for the small tree, and it is worth taking the time to look into trees that are limited in their final size. The Japanese are the masters of effectively using small spaces and they've long revered maples for this reason, as well as for their splendid colour. Research trees that will suit both the look and scale of your garden; this avoids the heartache you'll otherwise face later of having to choose light over privacy when a tree has outgrown a garden.

Be aware that garden books are only an indicator. You need to find out how a variety will perform in your area. Will it grow quickly or slowly? You may need to investigate what root stock a fruit tree has been grown on as the same variety of fruit will reach a different size depending on the type of tree it has been grafted to.

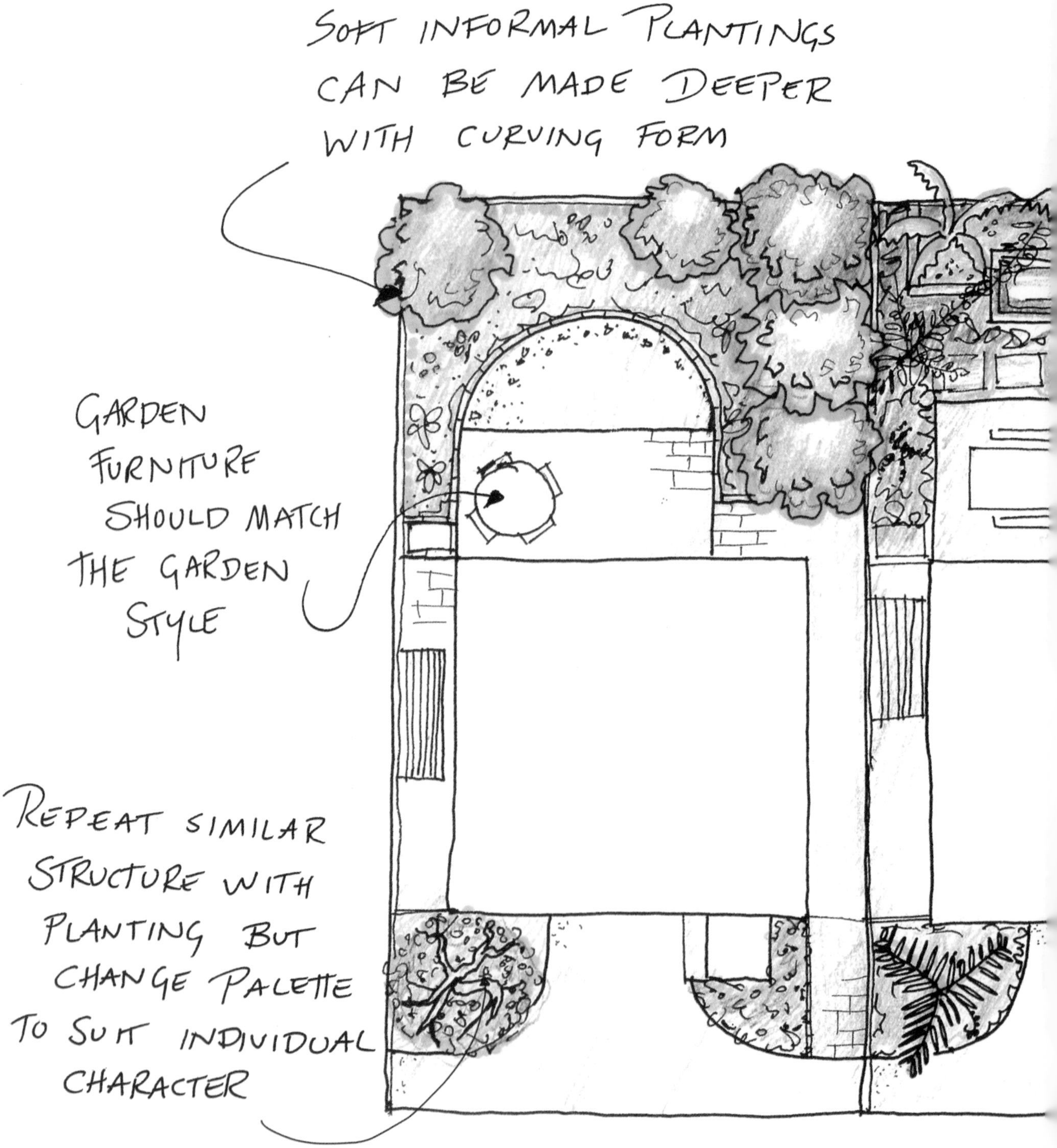

SOFT INFORMAL PLANTINGS
CAN BE MADE DEEPER
WITH CURVING FORM

GARDEN
FURNITURE
SHOULD MATCH
THE GARDEN
STYLE

REPEAT SIMILAR
STRUCTURE WITH
PLANTING BUT
CHANGE PALETTE
TO SUIT INDIVIDUAL
CHARACTER

CREATE A CONTEMPORARY
LOOK WITH SIMPLE STRUCTURE
AND LAYERED PLANTING

PRODUCTIVE GARDEN,
IN A SMALL SPACE
PLANT HERB LAWN
(MIXED, EVEN).
USE STANDARD TREES
ESPALIER AND CLIMB
ON FENCES

EVEN IN A SMALL
GARDEN SPACE KEEP
OPEN ACCESS
AROUND SITE

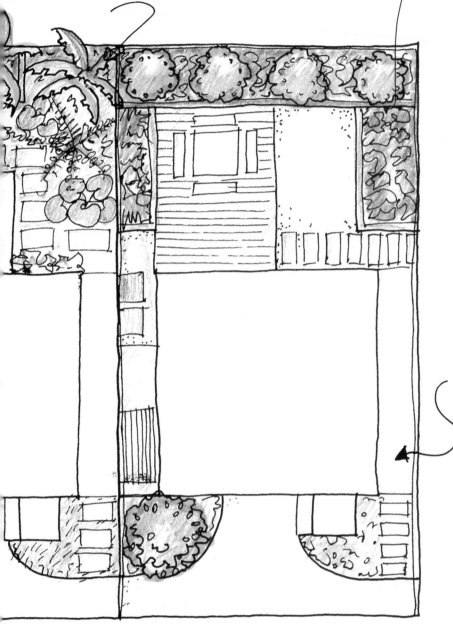

PLANT GUIDE

Rhopalostylis sapida
NIKAU
Our only native palm, slow
growing and slender. Perfect
for smaller gardens.

Acer palmatum
JAPANESE MAPLE
Popular for the wide range of
colours in its foliage. Also has a
compact, elegant form.

Sophora microphylla
KOWHAI
Dripping in golden yellow flowers in
spring, this slender tree is a food supply
for native birds. There are many varieties:
choose one endemic to your area.

Cordyline australis
CABBAGE TREE
The world's tallest lily, its flowers
are sweetly scented throughout
the summer months.

Meryta sinclairii
PUKA
This large-leafed tree will respond
well to heavy pruning, making it
ideal for small spaces.

Cercis canadensis
FOREST PANSY
This deciduous tree has heart-shaped,
crimson leaves that arrive in summer
after a flush of pink blooms.

Pyrus salicifolia
WEEPING SILVER PEAR
Weeping in form. Trunk and leaves
silvery, with splendid white blooms in
spring followed by miniature fruit.

Pseudopanax 'Cyril Watson'
FIVE FINGER
This dark green foliage makes a great easy-
care screen or backdrop in the garden.
Free-draining soil is ideal.

Magnolia 'Black Tulip'
MAGNOLIA
One of the more compact of the
magnolias, the flowers are deep plum
balls that appear on the edge of winter.

Camellia spp.
CAMELLIA
This garden classic is ideal for winter colour and makes a great flowering hedge when kept pruned after flowering.

Aloe spp.
ALOE
Growing into a shrub around two metres high, this aloe is great winter colour and food for birds.

Cycas revoluta
CYCAD
These Jurassic plants require little care as long as they are planted with a good potting mix and consistently watered.

Xeronema callistemon
POOR KNIGHTS LILY
Performs best in containers with a stony growing medium. Red plumes are formed in summer.

Astelia chathamica
SILVER SPEAR
Brilliant silver foliage. Grows best in free-draining soils or large containers.

Bambusa gracillima
CLUMPING BAMBOO
While running bamboos can be a problem in the garden, this dwarf variety is ideal for the smaller garden.

Agave attenuata
AGAVE
This sculptural form grows in a range of conditions. It self-propagates prolifically.

Ligularia reniformis
TRACTOR SEAT PLANT
One of the most dependable garden plants for foliage. Will grow from shade to part sun but needs plenty of water.

Asplenium bulbiferum
HEN AND CHICKEN FERN
One of the most reliable ferns. Easily propagated by planting the small pups that form on the mature fronds.

Liriope muscari
LIRIOPE

An excellent deep-green, thick-leaved ground cover with the added joy of a carpet of flowers in late summer. Watch the snails though.

Anemanthele lessoniana
GOSSAMER GRASS

This hardy grass is perfect for the fringes of a garden between shade and sun. Its colours change through the seasons from greens to rusty tones that capture the light.

Euphorbia spp.
EUPHORBIA

A great plant for texture and form. Comes in a range of colours from blue to silver, plum and yellow.

Loropetalum chinensis
CHINESE FRINGE FLOWER

A foliage plant with a compact weeping form that suits the small garden. Attractive pink flowers in summer on purple foliage.

Corokia spp.
COROKIA

These twisting divaricates add great texture to any garden and can be trimmed to any shape or any space.

Clivia spp.
CLIVIA

The best varieties are the reds and yellows, which have been bred for splendid colour and beautiful, thick, leathery leaves.

Muehlenbeckia axillaris
MUEHLENBECKIA

This hardy groundcover performs well in the harshest conditions, making it the perfect green cover through planting.

CONTAINERS

Buxus spp.
TOPIARY (BUXUS, BAY OR COROKIA)

Topiary is an elegant addition to any garden. Great for pots and can be used to give structure to informal plantings.

Cymbidium spp.
ORCHID

Best-suited to containers where they can be displayed at their best and popped into a sheltered corner when not in flower.

BONSAI

Even the smallest garden has room for a bonsai. This ancient art of pruning a plant's roots to restrict growth can also be achieved with many natives.

Solanum lycopersicum
TOMATO

Use containers to grow a range of food, including treats like cherry tomatoes.

OTHER PLANTS TO CONSIDER

Trachelospermum jasminoides
STAR JASMINE

Gardenia spp.
GARDENIA

Pratia perpusilla
PRATIA

Libertia grandiflora
MIKOIKOI

Leptinella spp.
COTULA

Plumeria spp.
FRANGIPANI

For warmer gardens, this is the king of all fragrance, with immaculate wax-like flowers in the heart of summer.

Pelargonium spp.
GERANIUM

Have long been a favourite container plant, flowering for extended periods and easily propagated from cuttings.

Narcissus spp.
BULBS (HYACINTH, DAFFODIL OR TULIP)

Bulbs such as daffodils are a great way to capture the change of season in a garden and are also fun for children.

Fragaria x *ananassa*
STRAWBERRY

Strawberries are highly productive in containers or grow in vertical units. Give them plenty of food and water.

THE NATURAL
Collector's
Garden

A garden can be an art form, a watercolour of plants, a sculpted room of green, and for some a gallery in which the artistry of nature is arranged plant by plant. This is the collector's garden, the creation of horticulturalists driven, well, by particular enthusiasms that some may say run into obsessions!

▲ **PREVIOUS PAGES** The banana lotus is a grand example of the extraordinary plants that are so peculiar and alluring that they are hard to resist.

Bromeliads have long been favoured by collectors. This red nerogelia was one of the first bromeliads I planted in my parents' garden.

▶ **RIGHT** The Auckland garden of artist Michael Shepherd, who collects not just native plants that others may overlook (his garden includes puha and the grass microleana) but also native insects. A tower in the front garden is home to native cockroach species which he was gifted by a friend on a significant birthday.

ON THE FRINGES of this 'club' are the true enthusiasts who have been overcome by their passions. Hidden in ordinary suburban backyards are greenhouses packed with superb collections that range from exotic orchids to begonias grown to be brought out to show once, maybe twice a year, and alpine plants, some which may be one of two or three in the country. Most collectors are members of plant societies, whose members trade and share seeds, cuttings, and the secrets of growing these gems. These societies are always on the lookout for new members. Not only does joining provide you with an opportunity to share in some valuable knowledge, it is also an opportunity to develop a collection of your own. At most meetings, which are more often than not held monthly, there will be a plant-trading table where members of the society bring different varieties along for other members to swap and try.

As you prove your mettle and your worth you'll find that more and more interesting plants will come your way. With little new plant material coming into the country, and most of these plants being true collectors' pieces that need to be maintained under glass, these backyard collections are like forgotten libraries. If you have even a skerrick of the 'collector gene', your interest in these rare plants could help preserve them so other generations can get to know them.

Collections generally start when a gardener has an interest in a particular plant, an interest that grows and grows. I've met iris growers, fern specialists and bromeliad lovers, as well as gardeners such as those at Texture Plants in Christchurch, whose broad collection includes the most wonderful and suitable garden plants from here and abroad.

It is easy to become fixated on the plants themselves and you can lose sight of the best way to present them. And presentation is everything.

It comes down to organisation, which may in fact make the plants easier to care for. If you can imagine your garden as a slice of bush where these plants were first discovered, or perhaps as the face of a cliff, and can then recreate this environment with its hot spots and

damp spots, you are well under way. You will also need plants that will form a backdrop to your 'stars', be they large sweeps of groundcover or fresh green ferns. These are the neutrals that set the scene for the orchestration that follows. Some parts of your collection will feature one, two or perhaps even three plants, but other parts may feature greater numbers. These should be laid out first. Then add your details in the cracks and crevices or as highlights on a sun-kissed bed. You can arrange them according to colour or species or even the country of origin.

Plants are not only the 'furnishings' of our outdoor spaces, they also, with careful planning, form a significant part of the structure.

There is a good reason for organising the plants this way. Collections stuck in pots don't really let us understand much about the true form and nature of a plant. By putting a plant into a context we can really understand its peculiarities.

However, if pots are more suited to, or even preferred by, your plants — as is often the case with epiphytic plants such as orchids — you may wish to be more creative in the way you display them. In Europe, walls are typically covered by geraniums in pots, evenly spaced. There is no reason a collection could not be managed well this way, and in fact in an urban environment it could be interesting to do so.

The value of a plant collection is hard to measure and, of course, much of its value is in the eye of the beholder. I can't help feeling certain the more of the fragile diversity of the planet we manage to maintain, the better. Ironically, in the past the very act of collecting and trading plants has done great damage to ecosystems and so it's now our responsibility to preserve the remnants from here and afar, especially those we are sure are unaggressive and therefore won't escape into our wild places.

Design guide

RECORDS

IN ANY GARDEN, record-keeping is a great way of both learning and keeping stock of what works best. With a plant collection, be it rare, native or exotic, it is even more valuable. Keeping track of where you sourced the plants as well as their history is both interesting and relevant to how you will grow them. The further back you can take the record, the better. With many plant collectors now in their eighties, taking the time to preserve their knowledge is invaluable. Some collectors will even know where in the wild the seed was collected and who the botanist was. Using a recorder or even video to add these stories to your own library is well worthwhile.

Photos of each plant's flowers, leaves or other distinct characteristics should also be maintained so that plants can be re-identified should confusion occur.

LABELS

FOR A BOTANICAL COLLECTION to be kept in good order, the plants should be well labelled. This can be with discreet metal tags or you can be creative and design your own.

Keep in mind that they must be weatherproof and ideally have a means of being attached to the correct plant. This will vary according to plant species and can be particularly difficult if the plant is deciduous. Even on evergreen plants it is challenging to keep labels attached as plants grow and change. The more frequently labels are checked and realigned, the more effective this will be. If you have a map of your plantings then it is likely any missing labels can be quickly reattached.

PLANNING AND PLANTING

THE VERY NATURE of the plant collector makes it difficult, if not impossible, to turn down a new variety or variation but it is also your responsibility to find a place for your new plants once the thrill of the chase is over. I have met plant collectors whose glasshouses are like overgrown jungles; whose gardens require hatchets to cut through tropical vines and where trees have run rampant, even lifting out through the roof of the house. I've also been guilty of leaving plants in the garden still in their pots, waiting for me to plant them, only to rediscover them later with the roots growing through the pots, desperate to reach some real soil. Before we buy we must first till the soil and be sure our spade is sharpened.

Knowing your garden is also important. If you have boggy soil, don't be tempted by arid-climate loving plants that are sure to slowly drown. Either work the soil first or save that plant for another garden in the future.

CLUBS, SOCIETIES AND CIRCLES

IF YOU ARE to be a true collector it is well worth joining up with others. If you are looking for a group you are most likely to get the best information by contacting your nearest botanical garden. They have information on most registered plant collections as well as their own, and are often even the meeting place for local groups. They also have a wealth of resources and information so that you can become more familiar with your plants of interest.

THE NATURAL
Gardener

This might not be a 'how-to' book but it is about gardening. After all, a beautiful garden is one we want to be part of, counting down the hours until the weekend arrives and we can get out into it. Much of creating a beautiful garden is about getting the right plants for the right places, but it is also about ensuring you have quality soil that gets your plants off to the right start. After all, while we bask in its beauty above ground, beneath it all is a world of its own: creeping roots busily transporting water, nutrients and hormones, various varieties of wriggling worms, soil organisms, and many other wonders are all vibrantly humming away beneath the surface.

RIGHT FROM WHEN we first start planning our gardens, soil quality is important. And alongside watering it continues to be paramount as the gardens grow. Good organic compost, sheep pellets and blood and bone are the staples, as is mulching your garden beds. Some plants will need additional trace elements or lime, particularly if it's a productive garden. Good soil is also important for container plants, to ensure they are getting plenty of nutrients and that water is being dispersed adequately.

In addition to what we bring in, creating our own compost allows us to manage our own green waste in a sustainable way.

Compost

Compost is nature's way of completing the circle of life. Basically, anything that has lived once can live again and we can use this to our advantage, turning our kitchen and garden waste into a valuable source of fertiliser for our gardens. Having a home compost bin will save you money and reduce your household waste — and it is a satisfying task. Once you complete a full cycle of composting you will be amazed how much less rubbish you are sending off to the landfill, with waste that would have produced damaging methane gases instead becoming a primary source of nutrients for your garden.

I call my compost bin 'The Tardis': it never ceases to amaze me how much I can keep putting in and how a year's mountain of waste is magically transformed into three to four wheelbarrow loads of rich and valuable compost.

KEY ELEMENTS

AIR
Your compost bins need to have ventilation, so they should have gaps in the sides to provide oxygen, which is essential in the decomposition process. Turning compost will also help keep it well aerated.

LAYERS — GREEN AND BROWN
Think of your compost bin as a good lasagne. Alternate generous layers (10–15cm each) of green and brown waste with your additives in thin layers. See the 'Good composting' table (see page 300) to determine which waste is green or brown and which is an additive.

SUN
Warmth is crucial to activate your compost bin so positioning it in a hot sunny spot is important. If sunlight is limited in your garden, ensure your bin gets at least a good half-day of sun.

SIZE
Your bin should be a minimum of 80cm high and 50cm square (or round) to be really useful. It can be up to 140cm high and 140cm square. If that's still not big enough to cope with your waste, you need to run more than one bin. Multiple bins are great for large gardens where you have large quantities of waste. If you make the bins too high, they become difficult to manage. Making them too wide makes it hard to maintain good consistent layers.

MOISTURE
Maintaining moisture and adequate drainage is important. Your compost bin must be in contact with the ground so excess water can drain away. During periods of wet weather it should be covered, and in dry periods water should be applied before it dries out. Generally if you add a litre of water with each layer of brown waste, this will be adequate when the weather is moderate. Adequate moisture will be absorbed from the ground in wet weather. Never allow your compost to become slimy, and remedy this by turning it and adding more brown waste such as straw.

MICRO-ORGANISMS
If your bin is touching the ground, micro-organisms and earthworms will enter the bin from below. You

can encourage additional activity by adding a thin layer of soil in each cycle.

ACIDITY

Your compost bin should have a pH of around 6 or 7 to produce compost that is ideal for a vegetable garden. Without the addition of lime, your compost will tend to be more acidic than this. You can get a simple pH kit from a garden centre if you wish to be accurate but generally you can assure yourself that it is in balance by adding a thin layer of lime with each layer of green waste. (A handful or two sprinkled is adequate.) Fruit flies are a sign you are overdoing the green waste in proportion to the brown or have forgotten the lime and your compost is too acidic.

TYPES OF COMPOSTING MATERIAL

Compost materials can be divided into three main groups: green material, brown material and conditioners or additives. Green material is that which is high in nitrogen. It is generally fresh organic matter such as kitchen waste, seaweed or animal manure. Brown material is what I call the compost's bulk and consists mainly of dead or inactive organic material such as dead leaves, paper or mulched woody materials. Conditioners or additives include ingredients such as lime that keep acidity in check, soil that adds micro-organisms, or base minerals that will supplement your compost.

These groups — greens, browns and conditioners/additives — will help you keep your compost bin balanced. There are, of course, some materials that offer the key qualities of all three. Old legumes are a good example, as they provide bulk matter, high levels of nitrogen and other nutrients to boot. Consider these as bonuses and don't worry about making the composting process too complicated. It is just like a healthy diet: plenty of the staples and as diverse as the seasons provide.

Views on what should and shouldn't go into compost bins vary, but my rule of thumb is: if it didn't live once, don't put it in.

TYPES OF BINS

There are lots of different ways to build a compost bin, ideally using whatever materials are available for reuse. But avoid wood treated with heavy metals, and don't forget both a lid and ventilation. One side must either be open or easily dismantled so you can access your composted material. Some pre-made bins come with hatches at the base, allowing you to access the matured compost from the bottom of the pile while you are still filling the bin from the top.

The plastic composters available from your local hardware or garden centre are very efficient and tidy for the home gardener. They'd be my recommendation for beginners.

TABLE KEY

* CONDITIONERS OR ADDITIVES   Light dressings of the conditioners or additives will help keep your compost in balance and high in key nutrients. You don't need a lot of them but they are important in keeping your compost healthy (occasional dusting).

** GREENS   Use as much as you want, as long as the ratio is equal to or slightly less than the thickness of brown material (10–15cm layers).

*** BROWNS   Use as much as you want, as long as the ratio is roughly the same as your green waste. A light hosing with water will help activate the decomposition of these materials and should be applied after a layer of browns has been added (10–15cm layers).

GOOD COMPOSTING MATERIAL

SOIL*	A thin layer will help add micro-organisms to the system. Ensure you add soil from healthy garden beds where you have had no problems, as these can easily be transferred to your compost.
LIME*	This should be applied where a large amount of kitchen waste is used in your bin. Fruit flies are a good sign you need a handful or two of lime. If you are happy to spend the extra money, use dolomite lime: it contains magnesium, an important mineral and one in which our soils tend to be deficient.
ROCK PHOSPHATES*	These are a mineral supplement worth adding to your compost bin as they add valuable phosphorus content, a vital element in the formation of chlorophyll and glucose. This will assist the 'fruits' of your labour!
WATER*	Your compost bin should not be allowed to dry out. Applying a light dressing with brown material should be plenty if sufficient green material is being added to the pile — but keep an eye on the moisture content, which should be around 40–50 per cent. Having a lid on your compost bin is a good idea, especially when rainfall is high, as too much moisture can be equally detrimental. It also helps keep animals out and smells in.
LAWN CLIPPINGS**	Try to keep the layers of lawn clippings thin and layer plenty of brown material between them. Thick layers of lawn clippings become hot and slimy and attract maggots. Keep to under 10cm thick.
ANIMAL MANURE (HERBIVORES)**	When adding manure, make sure you are balancing it out with plenty of fodder materials and lime, to prevent your compost from becoming too acidic.
FRESH PLANT MATERIAL**	As long as they are not diseased, any leftovers from your garden will be welcomed in your compost (see Weeds, page 301).

PRUNINGS**	Light prunings from hedges and shrubs are excellent composting material.
COFFEE GROUNDS**	These help make delicious-smelling compost.
KITCHEN WASTE**	Keeping a compost bucket under the kitchen sink will provide your compost with nutrients that are as varied as your diet. The more different colours of fruit and vegetable scraps going into your bin, the richer the end product.
EGGSHELLS**	These add a good source of calcium to your compost. They are often slower to break down and will be still visible when you dig them into the soil, but they will continue to add traces of calcium as they are crushed into the earth.
SEAWEED**	Seaweed is a great source of nutrients and helps also to accelerate the composting process. Do your research before you go gathering seaweed from beaches, though, as it is of course an important part of the coastal ecosystem. Wash off the salt before using.
SOME WEEDS**	Weeds are great for the compost but avoid tenacious weeds that will grow from cuttings. Wandering jew is particularly bad in compost bins as it thrives in the warm dark conditions. Avoiding grasses and weeds in seed is recommended, but if your compost bin is truly firing, it should be hot enough to kill many of these off.
TOUGH PLANT STEMS***	Heavier woody material is fine, but remember: the thicker the stem, the longer it will take to break down. Restricting to no bigger than a fat thumb is a good rule.
ASH***	Ash from your fireplace is welcome in your compost bin. It is rich in minerals and the charcoal content assists drainage. Make sure it's from untanalised timber.
DRIED-OUT PLANT MATERIAL***	This is good compost fodder. Essential to keep your compost well balanced and healthy.
PAPER***	Ideally paper should be shredded before it is composted and it should not contain heavy inks or plastics.
SAWDUST (UNTANALISED)***	Sawdust is fine as long as it is not from tanalised wood.
OLD LEAVES***	Load these on as they are the perfect fodder to keep your compost healthy.
NUT SHELLS***	Shells from nuts are a great source of brown material but may be of more use as a mulch for pots.

WOOD CHIPS***	Wood chips from a root grinder or mulcher are an efficient way of composting larger woody material that has no better use.
STRAW OR HAY***	Especially beneficial when it comes from horse stables and has the added benefit of a manure dressing.

BAD COMPOSTING MATERIAL

ANIMAL (MEAT EATER) OR HUMAN WASTE	While it's true that where there was life there can be life again, the process of composting such faecal waste is slower and smellier and has sanitation issues. It is not suitable for the home composter.
PAPER THAT CONTAINS HEAVY INKS	If composting paper, be aware of inks and plastics from the printing process and consider how you feel about adding this to your compost. Research suggests it is not harmful but I avoid it to be certain.
PLASTICS	These as a rule won't break down and those that do are filling your compost with chemicals that are not suitable for consumption.
METALS	While some metals will break down, you don't really want traces of metals in your compost, especially if your natural garden includes a veggie patch.
TANALISED OR TREATED WOOD PRODUCTS	The chemicals used to treat many timbers are highly toxic and include arsenic.
PAINTED TIMBER	The chemical content in paint means painted timbers are also best left out of the bin.
SOME WEEDS	Wandering jew and oxalis are good examples of weeds to be avoided in the compost bin. Keep an eye on weeds that have gone or are going to seed, as these may survive the composting process if it is not reaching hot enough temperatures, Some grasses, too, have developed in regions where fire is part of the ecosystem so they have an inbuilt resistance to heat.
DISEASED PLANT MATERIAL	It is important not to recycle diseased materials: it is much the same as sneezing into your dinner!
MEAT, BONES AND FATTY FOODS	These not only create stinky acidic compost but also attract rodents.

WORM FARMS AND OTHER FANCY COMPOSTERS

Worm farms and other compost systems designed particularly for those who have limited space certainly produce high-quality fuel for your plants. Remember, though, that the worms are living creatures — so they need your attention like any other pet.

BUYING COMPOST

It is likely, especially when you are first starting your garden, that you will wish to buy additional compost or planting mix to get your plants growing. It is important to know what you need to be looking for, so that you get the best quality and value for your garden. Compost is the most important ingredient in your garden and so has a significant impact on the quality of your plants and produce.

SUSTAINABILITY

How sustainable are the materials the compost has been produced from? Materials such as peat are not renewable so should be avoided.

COST

Like anyone, I like a good deal but my experience with compost is that quality beats quantity. Use a brand that has been around for a while and is respected by your fellow gardeners. Have a look also at consumer tests that will give you assured information that the compost you choose is going to do the job.

WEEDS

Most quality compost producers do inhouse tests of every batch of compost to ensure there are no issues with weed contamination. Many gardeners think their compost is responsible for a new flurry of weeds as they dig it through, when in fact digging over a garden bed with new warm compost will often stimulate seeds that had been lying dormant. If you have such problems, contact the supplier: if they're a quality supplier, they can send you information to show you haven't been sold someone else's garden problems!

COMPOST OR GARDEN MIX?

If you think of soil in the layers that nature intended, compost is the layer of freshly decomposed or decomposing matter beneath the leaf layer, while planting mix is equivalent to a very high quality version of the top soil beneath that. Garden mix is most appropriate where you require bulk as, being fully decomposed, it will settle well. Compost is still active, so large layers may become hot and also will settle unevenly as different elements break down at different rates.

Fertiliser

Compost is the primary fertiliser required for your garden and a good rich compost along with loads of sheep pellets in spring, summer and autumn is all a garden needs to be healthy. Liquid fertilisers can be great for plants in containers, whose needs are greater.

TRACE ELEMENTS

Trace elements can be added to a garden or the compost bin every five or so years to ensure your soil contains a balance of different minerals. These will be recycled back into the soil as you compost old plants. This is especially important for productive gardens.

For general garden plants, the element most likely to be absent is magnesium, visible in the yellowing of leaves. Citrus, gardenia and daphne will all favour a dose of Epsom salts to remedy this.

LIQUID FERTILISERS

Liquid fertilisers, especially fish or seaweed fertilisers, are a garden's tonic. You can make your own but be prepared for some pretty heavy smells along the way. Quality mixes from the garden centre or even the supermarket are perfectly affordable. You can apply them as a side dressing or over the foliage, allowing the nitrogen to be absorbed directly into the leaves and giving the plant a generous hit.

LIME

Not a fertiliser as such, lime should be regularly applied at the same time as composting in vegetable gardens but is not generally needed in your average garden. Most New Zealand soils tend to be slightly acidic and suit most plants. However, if you want to keep your hydrangeas blue you will probably need regular lime. Do a simple pH test using a kit available at your local garden centre. Though slightly more expensive, dolomite lime contains magnesium, which is a highly valued mineral good for citrus and vegetables.

ANIMAL MANURE

Animal manure straight from the paddock will give a fallow bed a welcome boost. If you are adding it directly, give it time to decompose before you plant again. Be careful about your source, as animal manure from non-organic methods may be full of the hormones and chemicals you've been doing your best to avoid. I prefer to add mine to the compost, to be shared throughout the garden.

SHEEP PELLETS

Sheep pellets, as a side dressing or dug into the soil, are a convenient source of animal manure, especially for city dwellers who may be without an affordable or accessible source of other manures. Check the packet to ensure they are organic if you wish to be sure your garden is chemical-free.

Mulch

A mulch is applied over soil to help retain moisture, lock in warmth, condition soil and reduce weeds. It is normally coarser than soil and acts as a protective layer. It also makes it harder for stray seeds to germinate and so will deter weeds. As mulches break down they add body to the soil. However, they can be less beneficial in cooler climates, when you wish to capture the sun's energy to warm the soil. Mulch will help lock in warmth but can also cause the soil to warm more slowly. In cooler regions, using a fine mulch such as compost will give you the benefits of both.

CAMBIUM BARK MULCH

My favoured mulch for general garden beds is a cambium bark mulch. This comes from the inner layer of bark, rather than the outer bark of the tree which breaks down very slowly and uses more nitrogen in the process. Cambium bark mulch breaks down faster and, if laid with blood and bone beneath, assists in suppressing weeds and retaining water as much as improving soil condition.

PEA STRAW

In my view, this is the number-one mulch for the vegetable patch and if the odd pea sprouts from your mix, this is a sign it's good stuff. Pea straw comes from pea bushes after harvesting, and is high in nitrogen. Buy in big bags from the garden centre and pile it on. As the mulch breaks down, it aids moisture retention and improves soil quality. It's a classic three in one!

SEAWEED

Seaweed is a great mulch for the garden but you need to wash the salt off to avoid burning plants. Apply with a nitrogen-based fertiliser: although full of trace elements and minerals, it is low in nitrogen. Blood and bone or sheep pellets are both suitable. Be careful, as seaweed's powers are potent and can be overwhelming for younger plants.

COMPOST

Compost, especially slightly coarser compost, can be used to mulch around plants. It is full of goodness but not as good at keeping down the weeds as other denser mulches.

PAPER

While some gardeners advocate newspaper as a mulch I would be careful that it doesn't contain heavy metals or nasty bleaches. I'm not a big fan of its looks either, so if you do want to reuse paper, put it in the compost pile rather than directly on your garden bed. Then your vegetable patch won't look as if you've dumped the kitty litter!

LAWN CLIPPINGS

Avoid using lawn clippings on your garden as they are too strong and are likely to burn plants. Save them for under the hedge row or the compost bin.

GREEN MULCH

The basic idea of a green mulch is the same as all mulches, to prevent weeds from taking over, to save water and to keep the soil healthy. It involves planting a vacant piece of land with seed while not in use. Plants traditionally used as green mulch have specific qualities, from using up an imbalance in the soil left by a previous crop to having long deep roots that bring up minerals and nutrients from deep down in the soil strata. This is why they are also effective in renewing depleted soil when used either as green manure crops (dug directly into the soil) or to make liquid fertiliser or enrich compost. It is of interest that in Dubai, where water conservation is of the utmost importance, research has found that the most effective method is planting incredibly densely as nothing loses water faster than bare soil or retains it better than a canopy of green.

Plant your green mulch in February and March. It will be ready to harvest at the end of winter (July/August).

COMFREY

Comfrey is most easily propagated by root cuttings in autumn, so if you know of a friend who has a crop and wish to give it a go let them know you're keen to help them dig it up. You will need to dig deep when you want to clear the comfrey out as it can be voracious, especially in a warm climate, so if you use it as a green mulch be warned it will take over in a prime spot. It can be grown in pots to keep it under control. It is a great option for orchards where it can be given free rein but not at the expense of other crops. The leaves can be used to make a rich liquid fertiliser or they can be dug into the ground when you prepare it again in late winter.

MUSTARD AND LUPINS

Mustard and lupins can be sown directly into the ground from seed. Go for complete coverage so that they will effectively keep the weeds down and soak up excess moisture over the winter months. If you are preparing a new garden bed, first lay old carpet over the entire area in autumn. After a month all the existing plant materials will have died off but if you leave it for longer it will be even more successful. Once the weeds are dead and gone, lightly cultivate the soil (never more than 10cm deep) and plant your crop of lupins. They will look amazing when in full flower. After enjoying the show you can compost the lupins by digging them directly into the soil and the ground will be ready for production.

Raised vegetable gardens

The benefits of raised beds are many. Lifting beds off the ground allows you to improve the drainage, define the edges of the beds and fill them with plenty of soil. The gains are even greater if you have limited space as you can keep your planting closer together, resulting in slightly smaller vegetables but more variety. The optimum width is between 1.6m and 2m, depending on your own height (you want to be able to easily reach into the beds from each side). A good height is around 500–600cm, making the beds easy to work whether you are healthy, elderly, pregnant or suffering from back problems.

The soil depth encourages the roots of your plants to grow deeply, allowing you to water consistently but less frequently. You will also find that raised beds have fewer issues with weeds, especially when you start with a weed-free soil and keep the beds over-planted, with little room for them to set seed. Raised beds also look great, and allow you to integrate your vegetable beds into the design of your garden. Selecting a material that integrates with your own style will allow you to have a vegetable patch in any garden (chic city slickers included).

SELECTING A MATERIAL

Raised beds can be made out of all sorts of materials. Ideally you can recycle materials such as old timber (watch out for chemicals, though) or old bricks. Otherwise railway sleepers make attractive, chunky beds and natural stone looks simply superb. There are also a great range of kitset beds available; they can be put together with ease for those whose strength is growing, not building.

MARKING OUT YOUR GARDEN

Once you have decided on the design of your raised beds, you need to mark it out in the garden. First you should roughly measure and sketch it out on the ground using builders' spray paint, which is easily rubbed out with a gumboot if you make a mistake and is biodegradable. Once you are happy with your layout, you can set up string lines to give you a more accurate measurement.

PREPARING THE GROUND

You can follow a couple of methods to prepare the ground. You can skim the area with a shovel, adding any spare soil or grass to the compost bin or putting it into the centre of the beds. Lift as little of the soil as possible while removing all green material. This is the fastest method. If you are preparing in advance you can lay old carpet over the area to kill off any weeds, which can then be dug straight into the ground once the carpet is lifted. Allow a good six weeks before lifting the carpet to check. This method requires less labour than the first and is effective in killing stubborn weeds without chemicals.

If you were planning to plant straight into the ground, you can follow this preparation with the sowing of a green mulch crop or by digging straight in, adding compost and manure ready for your first crop.

LEVELLING AND FOOTINGS

To build your walls you will need to level the lengths along which they will be built. When building brick

or stone beds you will also need to prepare for the footing, which is a level bed of concrete that needs only to be approximately 10cm deep for a wall less than 1m high. The width of the trench should be three times the thickness of your wall, with the extra overlapping either side. This provides a stable base on which to build, ensuring your beds will last a long time without cracking. You should dig a level trench to the depth required, compacting if necessary with a heavy foot. If your soil is not firm you may need to dig 5cm deeper and fill the trench with base course (fine scoria grit), which you should level using a piece of timber. This can then be filled with concrete, again using a straight piece of timber to ensure the surface is even. You can easily move the concrete around with the wood while resting your level on top. You'll be able to take a reading while keeping your level clean.

If your garden has a slight slope, you may need to step the base of the footing at even intervals so the ground outside can remain softly sloping but your raised garden will be evenly level on top. Footings should be left to cure for a couple of weeks, if not four, so the base is stable before you build on it.

LAYING BRICKS

Your bricks can then be laid on a bed of mortar. The mortar should be the consistency of toothpaste and evenly mixed. Lay the first brick of each course without mortar, but for the second and thereafter, 'butter' the end you are fitting into the previous brick, then lay them up against each other so the mortar forms a flat even join. Your mortar should be 10mm thick between bricks.

Keep checking your levels as you lay, and adjust them while the mortar is still wet by tapping gently with the trowel handle. Setting up a string line for each course of bricks will also help keep each row level. Before the mortar dries, use either a pointing trowel or a wet cloth to give the joints a neat finish. Ideally measure the final size of your beds so they are equal to a set number of your chosen bricks, including the mortar joins. This reduces the need for cutting at the end of rows. Start each new row half a brick out from the row below, as a continuous line of mortar will create a weakness in the wall. This is called a running bond.

FILLING THE BEDS

You then need to let the mortar set for another three to four weeks. The waiting game! If the season is right you can at least get started sowing seeds for your new beds. Fill two-thirds with topsoil or a high-quality planting mix. The remainder can be filled with compost, leaving 2–3cm at the top so you have room to mulch. Tap the soil down by stomping on it but don't worry too much because it will settle further over the following year.

Sowing seeds for the productive garden

One of the great advantages of growing from seed is the expansive palette of new plants that will open up to you. Rather than being bound by whatever is on the shelves at your local garden centre you can plan ahead yourself. Even better, if you are lucky enough to have a greenhouse you can grow things out of season or get an early crop of tomatoes under way.

WHERE TO BEGIN

Your first decision is whether to direct-sow. With vegetables this involves sowing the seeds directly into the garden rather than sowing them first into seed trays. This decision normally is dependent on the crop you are growing, with some performing better if sown directly into the ground and others best started in a tray. Starting in a tray allows you to select the strongest plants, start seedlings in a warmer environment, or propagate slow-growing winter plants such as brassicas in trays that take up little space while your garden is busy with its summer crops. A tray is a more controlled environment and so can be helpful with plants that are tricky to get started.

Plants that prefer to be direct-sown are normally those that do not like their roots disturbed once they have established and that perform well when allowed to harden to outdoor conditions.

SEED-RAISING MIX

If you are sowing seeds in a seed tray it is important to use a specialised seed-raising mix. You can mix your own or purchase specially formulated mixes. A basic recipe for your own mix is one-third coconut fibre, one-third compost, and one-third coarse sand (use pumice sand from a garden centre as beach sand is too salty). Good commercial mixes contain other goodies such as Trichoderma, a fungicide that protects your seedlings from root-borne diseases. You can of course add these yourself, but unless you are doing seed-raising on a large scale it is probably more cost-effective to buy a pre-made mix.

Wear gloves and a mask when preparing your mixes as there is some risk of legionnaires' disease, a soil-borne disease present in some composts. The same advice applies to handling any bagged growing media.

GERMINATION

All that most seeds require to successfully germinate is warmth and water. All the food they need is self-contained and is enough for the seedling to grow until it forms its true leaves (the leaves that follow the first two leaves all seeds have when they push through the earth). Some seeds can be soaked overnight or even for a few hours before you sow them, to help stimulate them into growth. Watering well is key to maintaining this growth. That's why free-draining sand is important in your soil mixture; it allows you to water freely while reducing the risk of over-watering and potentially rotting the new seeds. Warmth is the other key factor and explains why seed growing in winter, with its cold soil, is likely to be least successful. If you wish to get seeds off to a head start at the end of winter, ready to be planted out as soon as spring arrives, keep them in a greenhouse or inside.

SPACING AND DEPTH

How deep and how far apart? The instructions on the seed packet should always be checked, as optimal depth and spacing vary greatly between different varieties of the same plants. It is never an exact science, so if you happen to push your seed in a bit deeper or not as far as intended, the results aren't likely to vary hugely.

It is a good idea to roughly know how long it is from the tip of your finger to the bend, or that your thumb's a generous 5cm, as it saves mucking around with rulers. Those rough measures are as accurate as you need to be.

THINNING

Thinning seedlings sounds highly technical until you've done it a few times. It involves gently pulling out all the seedlings in a row but the ones at the recommended interval; leaving one seedling every 2cm, for example. Thinnings can quite often be eaten in a salad so need not be wasted. Your fingers do the job best so don't worry about fancy tools.

PRICKING OUT

When your seedlings are ready to be planted on, either in a pot or directly into your garden bed, the easiest way to lift your seedlings without bruising the stems or tearing the roots is by pricking out. A pen or an ice-block stick is perfect for gently lifting the seedling up out of the soil.

OVERSOWING

Oversowing is not always a bad thing and it does allow you to select the strongest seedlings for planting out. If you have ample healthy plants you worry about wasting, why not share with your friends and family? An inexpensive and sweet way of doing this is to make little newspaper parcels that can be planted directly. Cut sheets of newspaper into 10cm squares. Take five sheets at a time, place your seedlings and soil in the centre, and gather them up into little bundles tied with twine. Your friends can plant them straight into pots without even removing the newspaper; it will slowly decompose away into the soil.

You may even want to get a seed swap system going with friends, where you all experiment with different varieties en masse and then trade off your successes. Either way, it is a great way of sharing your love of gardening.

SAVING AND STORING SEED

Collecting your own seed from the garden is something that can really make the economics of your garden begin to pay off. It's easy to collect from both flowers and productive plants like beans and tomatoes, so I would recommend starting out with these popular crops. Good plants to start with are beans, poppies or karaka.

FOR NATIVES

Many natives are easily grown from seed. The seeds of plants such as karaka, corokia or puriri are naturally distributed by birds. You are best to first

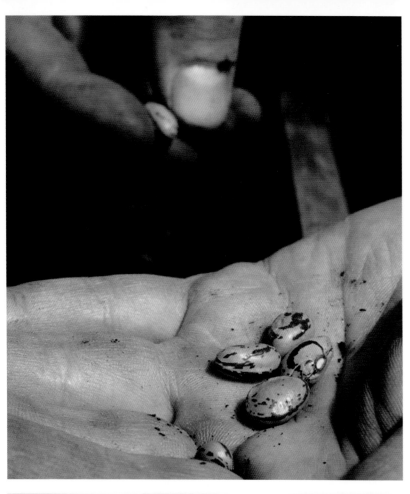

crush the seeds and keep them in the fridge over winter.

When planting them, the trick is to not bury them until they begin to sprout when you can then cover them gently.

FOR TOMATOES

First select the strongest and tastiest plant from your harvest and choose a healthy juicy fruit. Cut this in half and squeeze the contents into a jar with 2cm of water. Leave this for a day or two until it becomes cloudy and then strain it through a muslin cloth. The seeds can then be placed on a paper towel on a sunny windowsill to dry. When they are totally dry, scrape them off into an envelope for storage, labelling it with the date and the type of seed.

FOR BEANS

Towards the end of the season, tie a ribbon around one healthy plant and stop harvesting. Leave the pods to dry on the plant. Once the pods rattle, your bean seed is ready to harvest. Remove the pods and store the seeds in a dry paper bag until ready for planting. While there are different tricks of the trade for different plants, the basic principle is that you should collect your seed from superior plants that have shown high production, resistance to disease, and excellent flavour. The seeds need to be dried after the fruit or flower is fully matured and then stored in a dry cool place until the following season.

INDEX AND
ACKNOWLEDGEMENTS

Index

Page references in bold refer to illustrations

abutilon (lantern flower) 55, 69
Acer spp. 41, **216**, **280**
achillea **38**, **232**
African daisy **168**
agave 168, 169, **191**, **192**, **281**
ajuga **67**
akakiore 259
akeake **141**, 169, 259
allium 41, **97**, 99
almonds 233
aloe **117**, 169, **193**, **281**
alpine hard fern **116**
alstroemeria **40**
amaranth **96**
amaryllis 69
American foulbrood 225
amole **168**
anemanthele 38, 218
 Anemanthele lessoniana **40**, *244*,
 257, **282**
anemone **41**
apples 79, **98**, 276
apricots 99
Arctotis — *see* African daisy
argyranthemum **38**, **192**
Armeria spp. 41, **191**
artichoke, globe **97**, **230**
astelia 41, **142**, **167**, 219, **281**
Auckland Botanic Gardens **24**, **33**
Austrofestuca littoralis 167
autumn sedum **38**, **116**, **190**
azalea **217**

baby's tears **69**
bamboo **281**
banana 50, **66**, 267
Bangalow palm **66**, 267
banksia, creeping **167**, **193**
barberry, Japanese 219
basil **97**
bay 281
beans **99**
 saving seed 311, 313
bees 8, 11, 20, 38, 39, 93, 96, 104, 140,
 190, 221–33
begonias 110, 117, 288
bergamot **96**
bergenia 69
berries
 *attractive to wildlife 49, 140, 141, 168,
 247, 248*
 growing edible berries 85, 117, **231**,
 282
 poisonous berries **168**
bird of paradise **68**, **192**
black locust (*Robinia* spp.) 219
Blanc, Patrick 15, 104–5, 110, **111**
Blechnum spp. **115**, **116**, **140**, **257**, **259**;
 see also ferns
blood grass **68**
blood lilies 55
blue marguerite **167**, **190**

blue star creeper 259
bog sage 230
bonsai **283**
borage 99, **232**
bottlebrush 193, 233
brassica **98**, 99, **232**, 310
bromeliads **68**, 69
broom, native — *see* carmichaelia
Brown, Capability 121–22
Brussels sprouts **98**
Buddleia spp. 99
bulbs **219**, **283**; *see also* daffodil;
 gladioli; jonquil; tulip
butterfly bush 99
button fern **115**, **259**
Buxus spp. **282**

cabbage 231
cabbage tree 8, **140**, 228, **230**, 238, 248,
 250, 267
 mountain cabbage tree 69
cactus 181
calendula 93, **96**
California poppy 169
calliandra **216**
cambium bark mulch 305
camellia 217, **281**
cannas **40**, 55, **68**, **218**
Cape aloe **117**
Cape daisy **168**, **190**
capsicum 99
cardinal flower **68**, **218**
Carex spp. 117, **142**, 169; *see also* sedge;
 tussock
carmichaelia (New Zealand broom)
 169, **191**, 250, **258**
carrots 99
catmint 227, **231**
Celmisia spp. **168**, 241
chamomile 90, **97**
Chatham Island forget-me-not 23,
 168, 244
Chatham Island geranium **117**, **258**
chemicals and pesticides 11, 20, 74, 77,
 134, 224, 227, 302, 304, 307
cherry pie (*Heliotropium*) **40**, **219**
cherry tree **41**, **216**, **230**
Chinese fringe flower (*Loropetalum
 chinensis*) 282
chives 41
cineraria 23
citrus 50, **98**, 177, 186, **230**, 304
Clarkson, David 238
clematis **123**, **257**
climbing and growing frames 79, 85,
 93, 275–6
clivia 41, **218**, **282**
clumping bamboo **281**
comfrey 88, 93, **97**, 232
 as green mulch 306
companion planting 77, 88, 93, **96–7**,
 99

compost 49, 74, 79, 82, 85, 157, 296,
 297–303, **299**, 304, 305, 306, 307,
 309, 310
 acidity 298
 bins 297, 298
 key elements 297–8
 micro-organisms 297
 moisture 297
 types of material 298, 300–302
 worm farms 303
cone bush 193
cone flower **39**; *see also* echinacea
containers, growing in 85, 107, 178,
 270, 274, 290, 296
 container plants **280–81**, *282*
Convolvulus spp. 41, 193, 233
coprosma 49, **117**, **140**, **141**, 151, **167**,
 218, 247, **256**, 267
coriander 99
corn 99
cornflower 233
corokia 41, **140**, 169, 193, 219, 244, 250,
 256, 281, **282**,
cotula **117**, 283; *see also Leptinella* spp.
cotyledon **191**
courtyards 186
Cox's fescue — *see Festuca coxii*
crab apple **217**
creeping banksia **167**, **193**
creeping fuchsia 259
creeping gunnera **116**, **257**
creeping pohuehue 69
crocosmia 41, **219**
cucumber 79
cushion plant **117**
cussonia **66**, 69
cutting grass 142
cycad **69**, **281**

daffodils 88, **219**, **283**
dahlias **38**, **217**
daisies
 African daisy 167
 blue marguerite 168, 190
 Cape daisy 168, 190
 gloriosa 218
 *Marlborough rock daisy 167, 192,
 259*
 marguerite daisy 38, 192
daisy bush — *see* rangiora
Dalton's Plantation gardens **6**, **9**, 15, **30**,
 31, 86–**87**, **89**, 172, **203**, **207**, **211**,
 240, **249**, 266
daphne 55, **67**, **217**
 New Zealand daphne 117, **258**
datura 66
Davidson, Geoff 243
daylily **68**, **193**, **218**
decks and patios 26, 154, 178, 181, 185,
 267–9
delphinium **40**, **232**
dragon tree 193

dwarf toetoe 169

echinacea **39**, **97**, **231**
echium **167**, 181, 193
eco-sourcing 132–4
Elements — *see* Rudd, Rick
elingamita 259
eryngium **231**
Erysimum spp. 41
espalier 79, 275–6
euphorbia **40**, **192**, **257**, **282**
 native euphorbia **192**, **257**

feijoa **98**, 267
ferns 23, 25, 41, 52, 110, 238, 241, 290
 alpine hard fern 116
 Blechnum spp. **140**, **257**, **259**
 button fern 115, 259
 hen and chicken fern 67, 193, **259**,
 281
 kiokio 116, **259**
 maidenhair 259
 mamaku 69, 206, **256**, *257*
 mountain fern 259
 rasp fern (pukupuku) 115, 259
 rosy maidenhair 115
 scented fern (Paesia scaberula) 140
 silver fern (Cyathea dealbata) 259
 swamp kiokio 115
fertiliser 55, 297, 304, 305, 306; *see also*
 manure, animal; seaweed; sheep
 pellets
Festuca coxii 117, 193, 241
ficus 69
firethorn 219
firewheel tree 69
fishtail palm 69
five finger 169, **280**; *see also
 Pseudopanax* spp.
flax 8, 93, 126, **141**, 151, **191**, **218**, 228,
 232, 238, 247, **257**
forest pansy **280**
forget-me-not 41
 Chatham Island forget-me-not 23,
 168, *244*
frangipani 49, **67**, **283**
Fraser, James 153
fuchsia, creeping 259
fungus 104, 107

gardenia 55, 69, **283**
garlic **97**, 99
Gaura spp. **40**
gazania 169
geranium **38**, 290
 Chatham Island geranium 117, **258**
 New Zealand geranium 116
gladioli **219**
globe artichoke **97**, **230**
globe thistle **116**
gloriosa daisy **218**
gorse 20, 125, 153

gossamer grass 218, **282**; *see also*
    Anemanthele lessoniana
grapefruit **98**
grapes 85, 186
grass tree 69
green mulch 88, 97, 306, 307
greenhouses 90, 109, 198, 288, 310
green-wall systems 79, 104–110
    green-wall plants **115**, *117*
grevillea **193**
griselinia **66**, 244, 267; *see also* kapuka
ground morning glory 41, 233
gunnera, creeping **116**, **257**

Hanly, Gil **58**
hebe **142**, 250
hedging 11, 29, 148, 161, 202, 205, 244,
    267, 273
    hedging plants **66**, **68**, **98**, *161*, **166**,
    216, **256**, *267*, **282**,
helenium **38**, **190**
Heliotropium arborescens — *see* cherry
    pie
Helleborus spp. **41**
hen and chicken fern **67**, 193, **259**, **281**
hens 85
heuchera 117
hibiscus 49, 55, **67**, **216**
    native hibiscus 250, **258**
Himalayan white birch **216**
Hinewai — *see* Wilson, Hugh
hollyhocks 97
hostas **41**, 110, 117
houhere (*Hoheria populnea*) **141**
houpara **66**
hyacinth **219**, 282
hydrangeas **40**, **217**
hydroponics 79, 104, 110

iceplant **116**
    New Zealand iceplant **117**, *169*
iris **38**, **217**
    New Zealand iris (Libertia spp.) *117*,
    167, *241*, *259*, *283*

Japanese anemone **41**
Japanese barberry 219
Japanese maple **216**, 238, 267, **280**
Jarman, Derek (Prospect Cottage) 148,
    149, 151
jasmine 20
    star jasmine 69, *283*
Jekyll, Gertrude 19
Jerusalem sage 193
jointed twig rush 142, 169
jonquil **219**

kaka beak 49, **167**, 248, **256**
kangaroo paws 178, **191**
kanuka **141**
kapuka 49, **66**, 244
kapungawha 142
karaka **166**, 228
karo (*Pittosporum crassifolium*) **141**
kauri 153
kawakawa 49
    Three Kings kawakawa **256**
Kent, William 121
king of the bromeliads 69
kiokio **116**, **257**

kiwifruit 85
Kniphofia 41, 219
knobby club rush **142**
kopakopa — *see* Chatham Island forget-
    me-not
korokio — *see* corokia
kowhai 240, 250
    prostrate (dwarf) kowhai (Sophora
    prostrata) 238, **257**
    Sophora 'Dragon's gold' 166
    Sophora microphylla 141, **256**, **280**
Krüger, Ralf **75**, *170*, **179**, **183**, **184**,
    187, **194**, **208**, **242**, **268**
kumara 99

lamb's ears **39**,
lancewood 169, **256**; *see also*
    Pseudopanax spp.
lantern flower (abutilon) 55, 69
Larnach Castle **159**, **160**
lavender **39**, **96**, *169*, **191**, 224, **231**
lawn alternatives 23, 55, 88, 174–7
    remuremu (Selliera radicans) **68**, **116**,
    238, **258**
lawn clippings — *see* mulch
legionnaires' disease 310
lemonwood (*Pittosporum tenuifolium*)
    233
Leptinella spp. **117**, 244, **283**
lettuce 99, 104, 178
leucospermum 178, **191**
Libertia spp. (New Zealand iris) 117,
    167, 241, **259**, **283**
lighting 109, 209, 274–5
ligularia **41**, **67**, **281**
lilac 219
lilies
    blood lily 55
    cabbage tree 228, **230**, **280**
    daylily **68**, **192**, *218*
    Lilium spp. **39**
    Poor Knights lily (Xeronema
    callistemon) **117**, **250**, **258**, **281**
    water lily **217**
lime, addition to soil and compost 296,
    298, 300, 304
liriope **40**, **282**
lithodora 193
Lloyd Wright, Frank 253
lobelia
    cardinal flower **218**
    giant lobelia **68**
    lobelia 'Queen Victoria' **68**, **218**
    panakenake **67**
lobster claw 69
lomandra 69
loquat 50
lotus 60
love in a mist **232**
lupin 93, **97**
    as green mulch 88, *97*, *306*

mahoe **141**
magnolia **216**, **280**
makamaka 259
mamaku 69, 206, **256**, **257**
mandarin **98**
manila palm 69
manuka 20, 126, **140**, 141, **166**, **216**,
    225, 228, 230, 250

manure, animal 85, 298, 300, 302, 304
maple 41, 217, **216**, 238, 267, 276, **280**
marguerite daisy **38**, **192**
    blue marguerite **168**, *190*
marigold 93, **96**
    pot marigold **96**
marjoram 117
Marlborough rock daisy **167**, **192**, 259
Meryta sinclairii — *see* puka
Mexican bush sage **190**, **230**
michelia **217**, 267
mikoikoi — *see* New Zealand iris
mingimingi **141**
miniature date palm 69
miscanthus 39
mondo grass 117
mop top (*Robinia* spp.) 219
morning glory 20
moss (*Atrichum androgynum*) **115**
mounding 77, 79, 85; *see also*
    Muehlenbeckia spp. **166**, **258**
mountain cabbage tree 69
mountain flax **191**, **257**
mountain horopito 259
muehlenbeckia 69, 117, **166**, 218, 244,
    258, **282**
mulch 79, 82, 131–2, 157, 296, 305–306,
    307; *see also* green mulch
mustard **91**
    as green mulch 306
myosotis **41**

nasturtium 93, **97**
nectarine **98**
neinei **258**
nertera (*Nertera balfouriana*) **116**
New Zealand broom — *see* carmichaelia
New Zealand daphne (pintaro) 117,
    168, **190**, **259**; *see also* Pimelea
    prostrata
New Zealand geranium **115**
New Zealand ice plant 117, 169
New Zealand iris (*Libertia* spp.) 117,
    167, 241, **259**, **283**
nikau 49, **66**, 153, **166**, 241, 244, 248,
    257, **259**, 267, **280**
nut trees 88
    walnut 219

oioi **142**, **168**, 218
olearia 153, 161, **167**, 267
old man's beard 20
onions 41, 97
orange berry 117
Oratia Native Plant Nursery 243
orchids **282**, 288, 290
    native 238
Oudolf, Piet **10**, **14**, 15, **28**, **199**, 253

Pachystegia spp. **167**, **193**, 241, 259
palms 46–9, 67, 69, 126
    banana 50, *66*, *267*
    Bangalow palm 267
    cane palm 69
    fishtail palm 69
    fruit salad plant 69
    kentia **66**, *69*
    manila palm 69
    miniature date palm 69
    nikau 49, **66**, *153*, **166**, *241*, *244*, *248*,

257, *259*, *267*, **280**
panakenake (*Lobelia angulata*) **67**
paper, in compost and mulch 79, 85,
    148, 157, 298, 301, 302, 305
Parahebe spp. 259
    Parahebe jovellanoides 243
parataniwha **115**, **257**
parsnip 99
passionfruit 50, 79, 186, **232**
paths 77, 88, 90, 134, 137, 162, 201,
    206, 264
pawpaw 50, 267
pea straw 305
pears 77, 79, 99, 276
    weeping silver pear **280**
Pelargonium spp. — *see* geranium
penstemon **39**, **231**
persimmon **98**
pests and diseases 104, 125, 131, 225;
    see also chemicals and pesticides
    invasive species 20
    plants to control pests 93; *see also*
    allium; basil; marigold; nasturtium
Pimelea prostrata (New Zealand
    daphne; pinatoro) 117, 168, **190**, 244,
    258
pincushion protea **192**
pineapple sage **96**
pingao **167**
pintaro **168**
piripiri, scarlet 142
Pittosporum spp. **141**, 233
plum 77, **99**
pohuehue, creeping 69
pohutukawa 20, 132, **140**, 153, **166**,
    167, 225, **230**, 250
Poletti, Valda 238
Poor Knights lily (*Xeronema callistemon*)
    117, **250**, **258**, **281**
poppies **39**, 178
    California poppy 169
potato 85, **99**
pratia 283
Pride of Madeira **167**
primula, bog **218**
privet 20, 126
Prospect Cottage — *see* Jarman, Derek
protea **217**
    pincushion protea **192**
Prunus spp. **41**, **98**, **99**, **216**, **230**, 233
Pseudopanax spp. 66, 140, 169, 244,
    256, 280
puka 49, **66**, 244, 248, **280**
pukupuku **115**, 259
pumpkin 85, 99
purpurea **257**
putaputaweta **256**

raised beds 74, 85, 90, 307–309, **308**
rangiora **166**
rasp fern — *see* pukupuku
raspberry **231**
rata 169, 233, 259
raupo **142**
rautahi 142
red hot poker 41, 219
remuremu (*Selliera radicans*) **68**, **116**,
    238, **258**
restiad **39**, **218**
rewarewa **166**, 233

rhododendron 69, **216**
ribbonwood 244, **256**
Robinson, William 7, 11, 12, 19, 22
rock rose 169, 193
rose **218**, **231**
rosemary 41, **190**, **231**
rosy maidenhair fern **115**
rotational planting 49, 77
rudbeckia **38**, **218**
Rudd, Rick **150**, 151, **155**
Russian sage 233

sage
 bog sage **230**
 Jerusalem sage 193
 Mexican bush sage **190**, **230**
 pineapple sage **96**
 Russian sage 233
salt, effects of 82, 148, 158, 310
Salvia spp. **38**, **96**, **190**, **191**, **219**, 227, **230**
sand coprosma 117
satin flower 41
scabiosa **232**
scadoxus **68**
scarlet piripiri 142
scented fern **140**
sea holly **231**
sea spurge **257**
seaweed, as fertiliser and mulch 79, 157, 298, 304, 305
sedge
 giant umbrella sedge **141**
 pukio **142**
 spreading swamp sedge 142
 swamp sedge 142
sedum **38**, **116**, 117, **190**
seeds
 raising 90, 310–11
 saving and storing 311–13
Selliera radicans (remuremu) **68**, **116**, 238, **258**
sheep pellets 55, 157, 296, 304, 305
shelter planting 82, 85, 125, 132, 153, 161, 264
shore cotula **117**
silk tree 69
silver bush 41, 193
slender sweet flag **67**
Smith, Augustus John 153
snowball bush 219
snow clad 259
snow in summer 193
soil, conditioning 82, 148, 157, 296; *see also* compost; fertiliser; mulch
spider flower **96**
Spinifex spp. 167
stachys — *see* lamb's ears
star jasmine 69, 283
strawberries 117, **283**
sunflowers **96**, **232**
swamp astelia 142
swamp sedge 142
 spreading swamp sedge 142
swan plant 99

tamarillo **98**
taro 50, **67**, 110, 117
Tecomanthe speciosa 243, **257**
Te Kainga Marire 238, **246**

Texture Plants 288
Three Kings kawakawa **256**
Three Kings vine — *see Tecomanthe speciosa*
thrift 41, **191**
thyme 88, 90, **96**, **190**, **230**
toetoe **140**, 151
 dwarf toetoe 169
 mini toetoe 258
tomatoes 77, 97, **283**, 304
 saving seed 311, 313
toothed lancewood **256**
topiary 166, 256, **282**
totara 244
tractor seat plant (ligularia) **67**, **283**
tulips 282
tussock 169
 native 117; see also Festuca coxii
tutu (*Coriaria* spp.) 228

umbrella tree **66**

varroa mite 225
verbascum **190**
verbena 233
veronica 233, 243
vireya rhododendron 69
Vriesea spp. 69

waiuatua **257**; *see also* euphorbia
wallflower 41
Walling, Edna 25
walls and fences 11, 46, 50, 79, 161, 181, 205, 273–4, 276; *see also* green-wall systems
walnut 219
waratah **192**
water
 as a design feature 46, 56, 59–60, 154, 185, 275
 collection and reuse 79, 105, 110, 174, 182
 filtering 128, 142
 management 173–4, 177–8
 ponds and lakes 205–6
 retention 131, 148, 157, 185–6
 storage 181–2
 watering and irrigation systems 90, 107, 177, 182, 274
water lily **217**
weeping silver pear **280**
westringia 169
wharawhara **142**, **167**
whauwhaupaku **140**
whirling butterflies (*Gaura* spp.) **40**
Wilson, Hugh 122, 126
wineberry 142, 259
winter rose **41**
wiwi 142
worms 296, 297
 worm farms 85, 303

xanadu 69
xeronema 153, 250; *see also* Poor Knights lily

yucca **166**, 169, **192**

zucchini 79, **99**

Image credits

2–3, 9, 16, 18, 24, 27, 30, 31, 34–35, 42, 47, 51, 62–63, 70, 72, 76, 80–81, 83, 89, 91, 118, 120, 123, 127, 144, 156, 200, 207, 220, 222, 226, 236, 240, 251, 252, 293: Sally Tagg

10: John Glover/The Garden Collection, design by Piet Ouldof, Scampston Hall, image number JGT-GBORD-294

14: Andrew Lawson/The Garden Collection, design by Piet Ouldof, Hummelo, image number ALT G702 71 10M

28: Andrew Lawson/The Garden Collection, design by Piet Ouldof, image number ALT 482-8-1

44, 48, 53, 60, 61, 84, 106, 108 (both), 136, 245, 252, 284, 286: Zoe Carafice

54, 78, 92, 129, 130, 133, 135, 159, 160, 184, 239, 242, 246, 271: Steven Wooster

58, 150, 155: Gil Hanly

75, 170, 179, 183, 187, 194, 208, 213, 268: Ralf Krüger

100, 143, 196, 229, 260, 262, 265, 272, 289: Sophie Leuschke

111: Julie Dansereau/GAP Photos, design by Patrick Blanc, image number 0210343

149: Katie Garrod/Getty Images, image number 139810516

199: Steven Wooster/The Garden Collection, design by Piet Ouldof, Bury Court

284 image of magnolia 'black tulip' courtesy of Anthony Tesselaar Plants, for more information visit www.tesselaar.com

299, 308, 312: previously published in *Organic Vegetable Gardening*, Xanthe White (Random House New Zealand: 2009)

Acknowledgements

Many thanks to Judith Dalton who gave me the opportunity to work on the Dalton's Plantation project. Not only has the project been a great journey but it has also been supported by beautiful cooked lunches from the plantation café, and many coffees for the drive back to Auckland. I am also grateful you have welcomed my children and family and been a loving friend.

Also all the gardeners, especially Katrina Christison, who volunteered time to the project as well as paid work and travelled a great distance to be involved. Also to Fiona Henderson who travelled great distances to be part of the gardens.

The many other friends of the garden also should be acknowledged here: Andrew Boylan of Incredible Edibles, Anthony Tesselaar Plants, Verda, Beaumont Nurseries and Hinuera Stone have all, along with many others, contributed to the gardens.

Thanks to the team at Dalton's — Neil Dalton, Colin Parker, Mark Seebeck, Scott Bromwich, Graham Saltiel, Dion Edgecombe and Matt Dalton, as well as their support team Naomi Young and Sarah Davies — for the years of support on various projects that has been so important in getting me to this point. It is highly valued.

My thanks to Terry, Pam and Lindsay Hatch of Joy Plants, to Geoff and Bev Davidson and their team at Oratia Native Plant Nursery, and to all the crew at the City Parks Kari Street Nursery and Blackbridge for years of support and information.

Thank you to David Parkes and Rob Morrison of Tamata Holdings Ltd for the opportunity to work with their wonderful trees and exhibit with them at the Chelsea Flower Show in 2011.

Thanks to all the photographers involved in the book, but especially Sally Tagg, Zoe Carafice, Sophie Leuschke, Gil Hanly and Ralf Krüger who helped create the images that are so important in bringing the concept of the natural garden to life.

And thanks also to the Auckland Botanic Gardens and *New Zealand Gardener* magazine for their support with photos.

Major thanks must be given to 'the village' that has helped raise my children.

The parents — my mother and father, Judith and David White, and in-laws Lesley Dunn, Anthony Viner, Tony Dunn and Jan Coates — who look after us all and are surprisingly tolerant of being trapped and devoured by 'the otters' on a regular basis.

Thanks to the kindergarten mums Andrea Cocker, Jo Campbell and Elwyn Shehan (Ned) who undertook many spontaneous play dates to help get me to the finish line. Thanks to Auntie Linda for coming on board as a Super Nanny on many occasions. Thank you Rebecca Wadey for being a continued support in all the right ways.

Thanks to James Walkinshaw for doing everything, helping with landscape plans and couriers and photo archives but also keeping the rest of my life in order (at work and home) while the book consumed me.

Thanks to my very beloved husband, who is so tolerant of all my projects and gives me the freedom and support to be me as well as a mother. Thanks Chris for your patience and good humour.

To all our friends and whanau — Rowena, Jenni, Myke, Dylan and Sarah, Zoe and Will, Gillian, Christian and Kirianne, Sarah and Alex, Jacqueline and Myke, Lynda, Christine, Kahu, Teryn and Cath, Sophie L, Tina and Jasmine, The Biz Dojo community, Ru and Hamish, Clem and Zoe, Jacks and Paul, Great-Grandad, Jenni and Stephen Clay, The Macdonalds, Raymond and Jo, Johnny, Linda, Zita and Casey and David and Jane Margaret, Corbs, Kim and Sam and Auntie Margaret, Uncle Noel and Veronica — for the fun bits in-between. To the grandparents who are still remembered and loved.

Thanks to Gary Marshall for sharing his enthusiasm for permaculture (and his books) and to Mia for letting us rant.

Thank you to Ingrid Starnes for the creative collaborations.

Also another thanks to my mother Judith White, who has put in many hundreds of hours helping edit *Listener* columns and supporting my writing both by being an inspiration and a damn good critic.

Special thanks to Kelmarna Gardens and Framework and to the Unitec Sanctuary Garden for giving us access to their gardens.

And finally to Random House, the book's designer Kate Barraclough, the lovely Kimberley Davis, and especially Nicola Legat, who has been the most amazing editor. She could inspire anyone to finish a book, and has such integrity in her respect for the author's voice as well as knowing what it is a book needs to really work.

About the author

Xanthe White is an award-winning landscape designer. In 2006 and 2011 she won the Silver Gilt award at the Royal Horticultural Society Chelsea Flower Show and she has won supreme awards, people's choice awards and gold and silver medals at the Ellerslie International Flower Show.

In addition to her busy practice, which includes the ongoing creation of the rambling country garden Dalton's Plantation, near Matamata in the South Waikato district, she writes a column for the *New Zealand Listener* and *New Zealand Gardener* magazines, and runs gardening classes. She published her first book, *Organic Vegetable Gardening*, in 2009. Xanthe lives in Auckland with her husband Chris Dunn and their two young children, Jacob and Sophie Lee.

A GODWIT BOOK published by Random House New Zealand,
18 Poland Road, Glenfield, Auckland, New Zealand

For more information about our titles go to www.randomhouse.co.nz

A catalogue record for this book is available from the National Library of New Zealand

Random House New Zealand is part of the Random House Group
New York   London   Sydney   Auckland   Delhi   Johannesburg

First published 2012

© 2012 text Xanthe White; images as credited on page 317

Text pages 308–310 previously published in the *Otago Daily Times*, 'The Height of
Garden Fashion', Friday 25 September 2009

The moral rights of the author have been asserted

ISBN 978 1 86979 849 9

Design: Kate Barraclough
Cover photograph: Xanthe White
Back cover photographs (clockwise from top left): Sophie Leuschke; Sally Tagg; Xanthe
White; Ralf Krüger; Zoe Carafice; Sally Tagg

Printed in China by Everbest Printing Co Ltd